'PINCH ME NOT'

BY TONY BUGBY

Celebrating the twentieth anniversary of Oldham Athletic's sensational 1989/90 season

Daniel Publishing

First published in Great Britain in April 2010
by Daniel Publishing

ISBN 978-0-9565185-0-7

Daniel Publishing

Printed and bound by TJ International, Padstow, Cornwall

Foreword

By Sir Alex Ferguson

There are few of the successes we have achieved during my years as manager of Manchester United that have given me as much pleasure as the very first one in 1990. Defeating Crystal Palace after a replay at Wembley to win the FA Cup was a really wonderful occasion and it gave the club its first major honour for five years. It brought back the winning mentality to the club, provided a springboard to future triumphs and gave everyone a reason to celebrate once more.

It was a fascinating and challenging cup run, which saw us playing every one of the ties away from home. Nottingham Forest, Hereford United, Newcastle United and Sheffield United in the third to sixth rounds were all really difficult games, which produced traditional hard-fought, exciting ties. None of them were easy victories and that was also true of the semi-final, when we met Oldham Athletic.

We hadn't had what you could call a spectacular season in the First Division but most neutral pundits were confidently predicting that we were going to reach Wembley without too much trouble. Joe Royle's lads had enjoyed an amazing season in the cup competitions. Not only had they reached the FA Cup semi-final but they had already paid one visit to Wembley to meet Nottingham Forest in the League Cup final.

If my memory serves me correctly, Latics didn't have a particularly productive season in the Second Division – finishing in eighth place. I think I'm right in saying that Oldham's home record in the league was only slightly inferior to that of the eventual Second Division champions Leeds United but their away record was only marginally better than Bournemouth, who finished the season by being relegated.

I know a lot of people thought that Boundary Park's synthetic pitch gave them an unfair advantage because Latics played there on a regular basis and I have to say that results suggest that Joe Royle's lads had certainly mastered the knack of getting the best out of the plastic surface. They had some quite remarkable results during their FA Cup and League Cup campaigns. They put seven past Scarborough in the League Cup third round, which in itself is an amazing result, but even more impressive when you take into account that Scarborough had eliminated Chelsea, over two legs, in the second round.

Even more astonishing was their League Cup semi-final, first-leg win over West Ham. The Hammers were beaten 6-0 at Boundary Park and, despite making a really concerted effort to claw back the deficit in the return at Upton Park, they could only manage a 3-0 win and went out of the competition just one step from Wembley.

It was a similar story in the FA Cup, with Latics adding to their glories with famous wins over Birmingham then of the Third Division), Brighton & Hove Albion (Second Division), Everton (who ended the First Division campaign in sixth place) and Aston Villa, who were runners-up behind Liverpool. When we pitched in with our close neighbours from across Greater Manchester in the semi-final, most thought we had got the luck of the draw by avoiding Liverpool and Crystal Palace, who met in the other last-four tie at Villa Park.

There's no point hiding the fact that we felt quietly confident about reaching Wembley, but I remember warning that any team Joe Royle sends out should be treated with absolute respect. I'm not just saying that because Joe is a close friend, but because anyone who ignored his and Latics' record in the cup competitions that season did so at their peril. Thankfully, the authorities were sensible and decided that the game should be played at Maine Road, not quite equidistant between Old Trafford and Boundary Park but at least it meant both sets of supporters were limited to reasonably short journeys to attend the match.

Maine Road was a grand old and atmospheric stadium which provided a perfect setting for what turned out to be two fabulous cup ties. The original one went into extra-time after Ian Marshall had grabbed a late equaliser for Oldham. Earl Barrett had given Latics the early on before Bryan Robson scored to put the teams level at the break. Neil Webb looked to have scored the winner in the 72nd minute, but everything changed when Marshall found the net. The extra half-hour failed to separate the teams with both United and Latics scoring again, through Danny Wallace

and Roger Palmer, so a replay was required on the same ground a few days later.

I don't think anyone really expected to be treated to the same level of drama and excitement the second time around, but that's just what happened, with extra-time required once again. Brian McClair scored just after half-time to give us a lead which lasted until nine minutes from the end when former United player Andy Ritchie popped up to put his side level once again. Another extra half-hour was needed and I was beginning to wonder if this tie would ever be resolved. Joe Royle and his lads were displaying a resilient edge which was showing no signs of going away.

Anyone lucky enough to have been at both games will have wonderful memories because they were each contested in true FA Cup spirit with the outcome still unresolved until six minutes from the end of extra-time, when Mark Robins netted what proved to be the decisive goal. I was so delighted when that goal went in because I'm sure my nerves just couldn't have survived another replay against Joe's team. They were a total credit to him and themselves, (particularly full-back Denis Irwin!) and, if they had claimed the winner instead of us, it would have been totally deserved. But I'll be eternally grateful that they didn't!

Alex Ferguson

SUPPLIERS OF PRESTIGE CARS TO THE SPORTS INDUSTRY

- CONTRACT HIRE
- LEASING
- NEW CAR / USED CAR SALES

Tel: 0161-620-4000 / Fax: 0161-620-5000
Mob: 07958-549533 / www.vehicle-consulting.com

Contents

Acknowledgements

It has been an ambitious exercise to write and self-publish my first book, especially as publication has come only five months after I devised the idea. Just as Latics had a hugely successful side in 1989/90, it has taken terrific teamwork here to achieve what some thought was impossible. There have been a number of people who prefer to remain out of the spotlight, but who have been most supportive, so to them I say a heartfelt thank-you. Sir Alex Ferguson kindly agreed to write the foreword while Cliff Butler and Lyn Laffin at Manchester United also provided invaluable help. Oldham Athletic have been most supportive of the project, notably Gordon Lawton and Alan Hardy. The book would not have got off the ground without the help either of former Latics manager Joe Royle, ex-chairman Ian Stott and the players from 1989/90 who have all given me their backing.

I would also like to thank Stewart Beckett and John Hebb for the stunning design of the cover, Keith McHugh for his excellent help with proof reading, Paul Chan's technical wizardry and David Scripps for his keenness and diligence in trawling through the Daily Mirror's archives for the excellent photographs. Thank you as well to staff at Oldham Local Studies Library, where I spent many hours researching, notably in past editions of the Oldham Evening Chronicle. Gary Davies has kindly provided very welcome images of Latics memorabilia and there has been enthusiastic input from fans with stories and anecdotes for a chapter which greatly enhances the book. Finally, a big thank-you to Andy Vosper and his staff at printers TJ International for expertly guiding me through unchartered waters. It became a standing joke as we burned the midnight oil and corresponded through late-night emails.

The background

What made Latics' exploits of 1989/90 even more remarkable was the fact they were totally unexpected. Much of the previous season had been spent battling relegation, which would have seen them slip to the third tier of English football. Although they eventually finished 16th, it was hardly earth-shattering and the green shoots of recovery were barely sprouting.

Yet in the space of an amazing 12 months, Latics went from being an average Second Division side to the team whose cup exploits captured the hearts of the nation. Suddenly, they were defeating First Division giants seemingly every other week as they won through to the final of the Littlewoods Cup and semi-finals of the FA Cup as well as challenging for promotion.

You often get minnows having a lucrative cup run, but to have a club like Latics achieving success in both of the major knockouts was unprecedented. In addition, they were striving to regain their top-flight status after an absence of 67 years. It was no wonder a fan went up to Latics' manager Joe Royle in a local pub, declaring "pinch me" as he was scarcely able to believe what he was witnessing. Things like that didn't happen to little Oldham.

Those successes were even sweeter because Latics had experienced more famine than feast since the club was founded in 1895. It would not be an exaggeration to say that they had been starved of success, certainly in modern-day history. You had to go back to the era not long after its formation to find the most successful chapter in their history. They finished runners-up in the First Division in 1914/15 having also reached the FA Cup semi final in 1913. But for the outbreak of the First World War there is no telling what that team might have gone on to achieve as it appeared to be on the threshold of great things.

When football resumed after the cessation of hostilities, Latics were never the same dominant force and they were to lose their First Division status in 1923. Amazingly, it would take Latics 68 years before they were able to dine at the top table of football once more. In the intervening years there had been some dark and depressing days which is why the successes of 1989/90 were even sweeter.

In their long and not so illustrious history, Latics have only ever won three championships, two of which were before the 'pinch-me season.' There was a time, with George Hardwick as manager, when it looked as though the good times might return. It was under the stewardship of former England captain Hardwick, who was Latics' player-manager, that they won the Division Three North title in 1952/53, the first championship the club had ever achieved. Sadly, the funds Hardwick was promised to strengthen the squad never materialised and Latics were relegated 12 months later.

A lack of money has been a recurring theme throughout the club's history and when Royle was appointed manager in July, 1982, they were in financial peril – as he recalls from a visit by the bailiffs on the first day of pre-season training. There had also been times when results on the field put the future of the club under threat. The end of the 1950s were particularly fraught when they had to go cap-in-hand to the league in two successive seasons to seek re-election after finishing in the bottom four of Division Four. It was only through the good will of the other clubs that they remained members of the League in what were difficult and uncertain times.

When Jimmy Frizzell became manager in early 1970 after a distinguished playing career at Boundary Park, Latics were in danger of having to apply for re-election yet again. Frizzell, who succeeded former Manchester United and England legend Jack Rowley, performed miracles to pull Latics clear of the bottom four. It was Frizzell who laid the foundations for the successes of the Royle era as he took the club from the re-election places to becoming an established Division Two team in his 12 years in charge.

Royle picked up where Frizzell left off, eventually taking Latics to the next level – one which they could only have dreamed of. As so many of the fans could still remember the lean times of the 1950s and 60s, it was no wonder they savoured every moment of the Wembley campaign. Some clubs are so accustomed to success that they take it for granted. That has never been the case at Latics, where it has been sporadic. So when the extraordinary events of 1989/90 unfolded, it was something the fans embraced as they had never previously experienced anything like it in their lifetime. And the way football has evolved in the two decades since, it would appear there is very little chance of that level of success ever being replicated.

The 'pinch-me season' began a remarkable five-year period in which Latics finally reclaimed their place in the top division after an absence of almost three generations. They even created a little piece of history as they became founder members of the Premier League in 1992 and they spent three memorable seasons among the elite of the game.

They made a steady rather than spectacular start to 1989/90, which achieved lift-

THE BACKGROUND

GUNNING FOR GLORY.......Andy Ritchie, watched by skipper Mike Milligan, threatens the Arsenal defence in the Littlewoods Cup clash at Boundary Park.

off in November when they defeated reigning First Division champions Arsenal 3-1 to claim a quarter-final place in the Littlewoods Cup. It was one of those nights which minnows occasionally have and which are often regarded as a one-off freak result. That win provided confidence and self-belief that Royle's team of cast-offs and bargain buys could match any team, especially on their plastic pitch – something which was akin to having a 12th man.

It was only after the turn of the year that the season exploded to life as Latics achieved success simultaneously in both the Littlewoods Cup and FA Cup. They defeated First Division Southampton in an epic quarter-final in the Littlewoods Cup and Division Two rivals West Ham in the semi to reach a final of a major knockout for the first time in the club's history. In tandem was the FA Cup run which, after a low-key start when they beat Birmingham City and Brighton, also achieved a spectacular lift-off.

The mighty Everton were beaten after an epic fifth-round tie which went to a second replay and then First Division leaders Aston Villa were comprehensively

'PINCH ME NOT'

A SIGN OF THINGS TO COME.....but could Latics fans really have envisaged the delights in store as they embarked on the 'pinch-me season'?

defeated 3-0 at Boundary Park in the quarter-final. Latics were rewarded with a semi-final against Manchester United, which was not settled until after extra-time in the replay, when they were cruelly denied a second Wembley appearance.

It was a remarkable sporting period in the town as Oldham Rugby League Club almost made it to Wembley themselves, reaching the semi-finals of the Silk Cut Challenge Cup before losing 10-6 to Warrington. They were also a Second Division side punching above their weight as they beat giants like Wigan, Widnes and St Helens in the cup competitions. It was a memorable season as they also reached the final of the Lancashire Cup and won promotion in the Stones Bitter Second Division Premiership when they defeated Hull KR 30-29 in a dramatic final at Old Trafford as they tried to emulate the successes at Boundary Park.

They were heady days at Latics, who had never experienced anything similar in their history. Royle recalled arriving one day and finding three different queues – to the ticket office for Littlewoods Cup, FA Cup and League matches. It was a strain on a club who didn't have the infrastructure to deal with such success.

Chief Executive Alan Hardy, who was Commercial Manager at that time, pointed out that there were only two windows at the ticket office, so they decided to sell many of the 30,000 tickets for Wembley from the turnstiles to reduce queues which were still lengthy. He added that there was also a clamour for tickets for the two FA Cup semi-finals against Manchester United and also important League matches to complicate matters further. Luckily, the club shop, which had occupied a tiny wooden hut, had been replaced by a more spacious single-storey brick-built retail unit the previous summer with a £40,000 bank loan. The money, which was borrowed over a three-year period, was repaid in 12 months and the surplus from the season enabled a second storey to be added to provide office accommodation.

Mr Hardy added that by the time semi-finals and finals came around, the club would never have coped with the demand for souvenirs had the wooden hut still existed. He said: "We had people queuing in the shop and refusing to leave until we had received deliveries of Wembley merchandise, even though they had been told it wouldn't arrive for a couple of hours. When the merchandise arrived, we were selling it out of cardboard boxes as people wanted it so quickly. They were amazing times."

It was a whole new ball game to the club, who even chartered aircraft to fly supporters to the Littlewoods Cup quarter and semi-finals at Southampton and West Ham, something which would never previously have been contemplated. Press facilities at Boundary Park, which normally catered for a maximum of 19 journalists, were placed under increased pressure. Roy Butterworth, who has been press steward for almost half a century, had to commandeer a row of seats in the stand as an overflow as the club received up to 50 applications for the big ties.

Mr Hardy added the team's success helped the local economy and had the whole town buzzing. He said: "I think absenteeism was well down on a Monday morning because workers were keen to get in to talk about the exploits of the team the previous weekend. I also know circulation figures on local newspapers increased and the feel-good factor at the club had a knock-on effect throughout the town. I am glad we were able to have such an impact on the whole borough, especially for the fans who had supported the club for so long and who at last were able to lap up some glory.

"Nobody could ever have imagined that Oldham Athletic would play in the final of the Littlewoods Cup and semi-finals of the FA Cup in the same season. For a club of our size to enjoy success in one of the cup competitions would have been amazing, but to do it in two and also narrowly miss out on promotion was incredible. And it was a time when everybody was my best mate to make sure they got tickets for the big games."

Mr Hardy conceded that Latics overachieved that season and subsequently when they had three seasons in the top flight. He considers it almost impossible for them to repeat those cup successes now because the financial gap between the Premier League and the lower divisions has grown so dramatically. "I am not saying it cannot be done, but it makes it more difficult for lower-division teams," he concluded.

ROYLE RECEPTION......Joe Royle and the Latics team savour the outpouring of civic pride after they returned home from Wembley.

Royle reigns supreme

Joe Royle, Latics manager between 1982 and 1994, was the architect of the glory days at Boundary Park. Here he gives his personal insight into the unforgettable 1989/90 campaign.

"Twenty years later, I find it amazing how everybody still refers to it as the 'pinch-me season.' I am often asked how it became known as that. After games, I and a couple of directors used to go to a local hostelry, usually the Grey Mare in Royton. After we beat Arsenal, a fan wandered up to me in a bit of a daze. He remarked he couldn't believe it, and said 'pinch me.' We all had a laugh and a giggle with him, but suddenly it caught on and it was a good name as it was the sort of season the club had never had before.

There was a standing joke that the club had cup walks rather than cup runs. We would sit round the radio every year hoping for Manchester United home or away for the money to keep the club going, but invariably it was Hartlepool or Darlington away. Suddenly we were getting the big clubs and not only that but also beating them time and time again. They were heady days as we were doing it on two cup fronts as well as going for promotion from the Second Division although, in the end, we suffered because of the cup games.

I remember arriving one day to find there were three queues outside Boundary Park – one for a Littlewoods Cup-tie, one for an FA Cup match and one for our next League game. One queue outside Boundary Park was news, but there were three proper ones going up the road in different directions. It was an amazing time and, as I remember saying, if you could have put a plug into Oldham, you would have lit up Britain. The place was alive and it was great for fans who had never seen anything like it before.

It was an amazing season as it was unprecedented for a lower-level club like ourselves to achieve what we did. And nobody since has matched it. Burnley came close last season, reaching the semi-finals of the Carling Cup and winning promotion, but there has been no club firing on all three fronts like we did. What made our achievements even greater was the fact that there were no weakened teams in the cup competitions. Arsenal, Everton, Aston Villa and Southampton all fielded their full sides.

Much was said about the plastic pitch and the influence of it and, yes, we were good on it. What people conveniently forget, though, is that we had great away performances as well. But more than anything they were all top players, most of whom went on to play at a higher level. And some had already played in the First Division.

Our success in 1989/90 was a complete contrast to the previous season when we had been battling relegation for much of the time. I think one of the turning points was when Andy Ritchie and Frank Bunn were paired together up front. From the second they met, never mind played together, they were dynamite. They were, and still are, great friends. It was significant that in 1988/89, when we were battling relegation, Ritchie and Bunn hardly played together because of injury.

NICE AND FORGIVING........Denis Irwin looks on as wing wizard Neil Adams crosses at Wembley. The surface was different from the plastic at Boundary Park!

ROYLE REIGNS SUPREME

What was also special about the side was that the players got on well together as a group. They played and also socialised together and many of them are still in contact with one another. Wednesday was our day off and the players would go out mob-handed on a Tuesday. They could never figure out how I knew where they had been. Oldham, of course, is a small town and it soon got back to me. But they worked hard and deserved to go out and relax. I am not saying they drank to excess, but they went out together after training on Tuesday for a meal and a couple of drinks. There are invariably one or two who will stay out longer than others, but they came back in on Thursday and worked hard again. I think they were unique as a group in terms of how close they were. And I am sure that also had a positive effect on the pitch in terms of that togetherness.

They were also not scared to speak to one another in the dressing room. You always have leaders and followers, but in terms of leaders we had the likes of midfield pair Mike Milligan and Nick Henry, who were dynamite together, Rick Holden, Andy Ritchie, Andy Rhodes and Ian Marshall. There were no big-time Charlies and they would go into the same pubs as the fans. I don't want to make it sound like a pub culture, which it was far from, but they enjoyed a night out together and still do.

In the summer of 1989, winger Tommy Wright had left for Leicester and, whenever we sold players, there was always some money available to put back into the team, so I brought in Rick Holden for roughly half of what we received for Tommy. I had already signed Neil Adams, so we had two new wingers who were important in providing the supply for the likes of Ritchie, Bunn and Roger Palmer. I think when you look back over my 12 years as manager, we made a profit each season with our transfer activity.

There was no inkling about how successful the 1989/90 season would be after we made a slow start and didn't record our first win until the fifth match, but there was never a worry or a problem. Once we had registered our first success, we then won four matches in a row, confidence grew and we were flying. But though we were up and running, I did not expect what was about to happen.

I think the catalyst was our win against Leeds in the second round of the Littlewoods Cup. We seemed to play them every season in one of the cups and at the time had the evil eye over them. And we had also done well in the years leading up to this by signing four players from Leeds in Andy Ritchie, Tommy Wright, Denis Irwin and Andy Linighan. There was always an Elland Road element in the team which was desperate to do well – and the cup run started with victory over them. Leeds were favourites for promotion from the Second Division and the fact we beat them home and away was a statement as to the status and strength of our team. Our fans loved nothing better than beating them. Leeds is not that far away and they had a big fan base in Oldham at that time because of their history and success in the 1960s and 70s.

We were drawn next at home to Scarborough which was viewed as a potential banana skin, an awkward one, as they had beaten Chelsea in the previous round. It was soon far from that and they were demoralised as they could not handle the plastic pitch. It was a magical night for Frank Bunn, whose six goals in a game remains a competition record.

The players couldn't wait to get stuck into Arsenal in the next round as they were the reigning First Division champions and current League leaders. As for the fans, their attitude was 'It has been nice, but send the suits back' as they never expected us to beat them. If Leeds was the catalyst and Scarborough was a great night, beating Arsenal was the moment when people sat up and started to take notice of Oldham. It was a big statement.

That win put us into the quarter-finals, in which we were seconds from going out at First Division Southampton until Andy Ritchie scored an equaliser in the 94th minute. Southampton were unhappy at the length of injury time, but before the game referee Roger Milford told us he was not going to play any added time at the end of the opening half, but put all the injury time on at the end. I suppose it was exceptional and they certainly don't do it that way today. Southampton were twice ahead but Ritchie took a hand, scoring both our goals to earn a replay. I remember jumping out of the dug-out when we equalised and rather childishly shouting to their bench 'plastic, back to plastic,' which was to put it into their minds as I knew what they would be thinking. I knew what I was doing but, looking back, it wasn't very dignified for a manager. You need a slice of luck and we certainly had it that night.

I remember when I won the FA Cup as Everton manager in 1995, the only game we looked like losing was at Bristol City, who battered us. If Junior Bent had hit the target on any number of occasions, we would have been knocked out. As it was, we survived and Matt Jackson swung his left foot at a ball, which he never normally did, and we won the game. That's the cup and the Southampton game in the Littlewoods Cup was certainly important to us.

At that stage, we had a few bob in the coffers and the directors allowed us to travel by plane to Southampton which didn't please all the players. Ian Marshall and Andy Rhodes didn't like flying and this was an ancient charter aircraft. But nobody noticed the trip back as we were on such a high. I seem to remember a young man called

ROYLE REIGNS SUPREME

Alan Shearer coming on as a substitute in the replay and thinking what a handful he was and wondering if he was available. People forget Southampton were a First Division team then but the result was never in any doubt at Boundary Park.

We were getting crowds of over 18,000 for the cup-ties by this stage and the place was rocking. I would say the 6-0 win against West Ham in the first leg of the semi-final was the result of the season. For all the big games we played, I was worried the team might freeze on such a big occasion. It was Valentine's Day and I opened the paper that morning to see Mike Milligan in a gangster suit and holding a machine gun. I thought: 'Millie, what have you done?' My fear was that the feature would be pinned on their dressing room wall, but he didn't care. He is the sort of player I would want to be in the same trench with if I were fighting a war.

If we were chasing a game, we would go three at the back quite readily because we had the pace of Earl Barrett and Denis Irwin and Andy Barlow's adaptability and we would go 3-4-3. We had been working on our usual 4-4-2 with Ian Marshall at the back alongside Barrett. Marshall was prodding me in the dressing room about playing up front which he loved and I changed things round in the tunnel before we went out. I preferred him as a centre-half because he was clever, quick and good on the ball, and I would go as far as saying he might even have played for England at centre-half, but he got his way and played more and more up front.

I looked at West Ham's team, which included a sweeper, and thought 'Why not? Let's have a go' and we

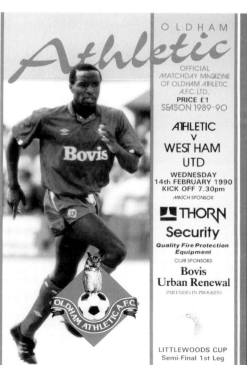

'PINCH ME NOT'

ON THE RUN.......winger Rick Holden goes rampaging in the sensational semi-final slaughter of West Ham.

went three up front against their central defenders. It wasn't a difficult decision as, whatever we had already achieved that season, it was done by going for it. We always played two wingers and were not a defensive side, relying on the pace of Barrett, Paul Warhurst and Marshall at the back. We were 3-0 ahead at half-time when I told Marshall to get back into defence as we were reverting to a back four. We scored a fourth goal immediately after half-time, went on to win 6-0 and it could have been an even bigger margin of victory, which you don't expect in the first leg of a cup semi-final.

The celebrations afterwards were as though we had already won the cup. And for the second leg, I could tell that the heads of the players were all over the place. They were already at Wembley which was something I could not deny. West Ham battered us in the second leg, scored three and I remember having terse words with the players afterwards. We were playing Everton in the FA Cup three days later and I told them we would be taken apart if we did the same on the Saturday.

We didn't even get to open the champagne at Upton Park. Director Rob Adams came in with a bottle, realised he was walking into a maelstrom, turned round and left. We were having words. We had switched off and I was not having that. We were better than West Ham, as we had proved by beating them in the league at their place and then 6-0 in the semi-final. Later, we defeated them 3-0 at home in the league.

The timing was great because it served as a wake-up call for the game against Everton, whom we beat in the second replay of our FA Cup fifth-round tie. We had kicked off our FA Cup run at Birmingham City who, in those days, were in the Third Division. And we so nearly found ourselves as victims of a giant-killing act. We would have been knocked out but for Frank Bunn scoring a late equaliser against his home-city team and also the side he supports. You will find we scored a lot of late equalisers and winners – and that was no accident. It was because we never gave in and the players were together as a team.

In the replay, we beat Birmingham 1-0 to earn ourselves a home tie against Brighton, who were in the same division as ourselves and who we also only scraped past. It was great for me personally when we drew my former club Everton in the fifth round. They were managed by Colin Harvey, who I played alongside for Everton and who is one of my closest buddies. I wanted to beat them, just as I had enjoyed scoring against them for Manchester City, Bristol City and Norwich after I had left Goodison Park.

They were three massive games against Everton and we did well in the first one at Boundary Park to draw 2-2, having conceded two early goals. In the replay at Goodison, Norman Whiteside was sent off and they were physical and set about us in a way they couldn't on plastic. That game also went to extra-time and a second replay. The amount of matches we were playing would eventually take its toll and would have a effect on us later in the season. All three of the games were close, but we managed to finally get past them and, four days later, we were back in FA Cup action, taking on Aston Villa in the quarter-finals.

They were First Division leaders and some people were saying that this would be the time when we received our comeuppance after scrambling past Everton and beating Arsenal on the plastic. But we were convincing 3-0 winners and Graham Taylor was magnanimous, saying "Don't get carried away with the pitch." He said we got the ball into dangerous areas more than any other team he had seen. Graham said while the plastic pitch helped us because we were good on it, the bottom line was that we were a good team.

'PINCH ME NOT'

We were playing games every three or four days at that stage and, with effectively the same players, it was terrific what we were achieving. Close on 39,000 fans passed through the turnstiles at Boundary Park in the space of those four days. The other thing was that the club just couldn't cope with the demand for tickets as we only had two little kiosks. I am not being critical, but we were simply not geared for success on that scale. And that was certainly the case after the Villa victory as we found ourselves playing Manchester United in the semi-finals, the dream draw for the fans.

Crystal Palace had beaten Liverpool 4-3 in the first semi-final played earlier in the day. It was a massive upset because Liverpool had beaten Palace 9-0 in the league earlier in the season. People were not giving us any chance, saying it would be a different story on grass as this was Manchester United playing little Oldham. It was probably the biggest season in Alex Ferguson's career as they went on to lift the FA Cup, the first trophy he won as United manager, because the pressure had been mounting on him. There we were slugging it toe-to-toe on the same, level playing field with Manchester United and we were terrific on the day. I still feel aggrieved by the refereeing of the game. We felt we were the better team and should have won.

We drew 3-3 thanks to goals from Barrett, Marshall and Palmer. I can remember his equaliser as though it was yesterday. I also recall director Norman Holden doing a jig on the coach after the game, such was his excitement. He was buzzing, as was the whole town. Three days later, we were back at Maine Road for the replay and another terrific game. We fell behind early in the second half and I pushed central defender Andy Holden up front. When Andy Ritchie equalised late on, Holden pointed as if to go back into defence. I told him to stay up front and try to win the game. We were in the great situation of having one final in the pocket and I didn't want another replay. If we hadn't already been through to Wembley in the Littlewoods Cup, there is no doubt at all Andy would have gone back into defence and we would have gone for another replay or to keep it tight and play on the break.

Sadly, there was a big hole in the middle of our defence in extra-time and substitute Mark Robins burst through to score the winner for United. When you are playing in the semi final of the FA Cup, it is hard to say the next league game is more important, but I wanted desperately to at least make the play-offs and knew some of our players were getting very tired. You have to bear in mind Earl Barrett played in all 65 games while Rick Holden, Andy Barlow, Denis Irwin, Mike Milligan and Nick Henry all appeared in 60 or more matches. I would say we peaked for the first semi-final against United at Maine Road, bearing in mind the opposition had Bryan Robson and company in their team.

For little Oldham to be playing at that level was incredible and I think the 3-3

WELL DONE, MY SON.......Earl Barrett is the toast of Oldham following his goal in the first Maine Road thriller against Manchester United – arguably the side's best performance of the 'pinch-me season.'

'PINCH ME NOT'

draw was our best performance. By the time we reached the final of the Littlewoods Cup, we were over the top. Ian Marshall was ruled out through injury while Irwin, Henry and Bunn were all carrying knocks. We had played 60 games and it had started to take its toll. In saying that, I recently looked at the video of the final against Nottingham Forest and we did much better than I thought. My son Darren is European sales manager for ProZone and he has done the analysis on that game which we did not have in those days. We had more shots than Forest and put in more crosses.

I hadn't bothered too much about the final because, although it was not a bad memory, it was not a great one either. That reminded me of something David Pleat, who was manager of Tottenham, once told me. He said when you look at the video of a match on the Monday morning, it is usually not as bad as you thought it was or, in some cases, not as good. I stayed away from looking at the video again, but it was not as bad as I thought and we more than held our own as Forest were a top team at that time.

I think getting to Wembley was more important for the fans than winning. We wanted to win but, if you had promised me then the League Cup final or making the play-offs, it would not have been an instant 'let's win the cup.' For the betterment of the club, it was more important to win promotion. On the day of the final, we didn't lack effort or honesty, but we weren't at our strongest. We were tired.

The build-up was hard because we played and lost five days earlier at Portsmouth, where Andy Holden picked up an injury which cruelly kept him out of the final. It was a shame because he had played an important part in the turnabout in the club's fortunes. I also had a big decision to make as to the goalkeeping position. I felt big Jon Hallworth had lacked confidence in the two FA Cup semi-finals against Manchester United and I instead went for Andy Rhodes. It was hard on Jon because he had played his part and there was little to separate the two. Andy was the better shot-stopper while Jon had the edge on claiming crosses and kicking. Though we lost 1-0, I felt Andy's performance justified what I did as he was arguably our best player.

Having played Portsmouth, we didn't have a lot of time to prepare for the final. We had played so many games that we weren't training much. We were having warm-ups which involved a little bit of running and a lot of stretching, plus plenty of head tennis and a little work on the shape of the team. We had done a deal with my friend Phil Black, who was a tailor, and we all had new suits. The players thought it was great. This was Oldham feeling important. It was great driving to the game to be confronted by a sea of blue and white on Wembley Way and also when we walked on to the pitch.

INFORMATION

TEAM SHEET

OLDHAM ATHLETIC	NOTTINGHAM FOREST
1. ANDY RHODES	1. STEVE SUTTON
2. DENNIS IRWIN	2. BRIAN LAWS
3. ANDY BARLOW	3. STUART PEARCE
4. NICK HENRY	4. DES WALKER
5. EARL BARRETT	5. STEVE CHETTLE
6. PAUL WARHURST	6. STEVE HODGE
7. NEIL ADAMS	7. GARY CROSBY
8. ANDY RITCHIE	8. GARRY PARKER
9. FRANK BUNN	9. NIGEL CLOUGH
10. MIKE MILLIGAN	10. NIGEL JEMSON
11. RICK HOLDEN	11. FRANZ CARR
12. ROGER PALMER	12. TERRY WILSON
14. GARY WILLIAMS	14. TOMMY GAYNOR

WEMBLEY VENUE OF LEGENDS

WEMBLEY STADIUM LIMITED, WEMBLEY, HA9 0DW
TELEPHONE: 01-902 8833 • FAX: 01-900 1055

As for the game, nobody let us down in terms of missing ridiculous chances and we had a go. Forest manager Brian Clough was complimentary, saying something like 'Hey, young man, you had a fantastic season, you have good players and your team are a credit to you.' He invited me for a beer which we had in the Forest dressing room while their players were still out on the pitch acknowledging their supporters. We had a general chat about football and he was lovely and very gracious as you can be in victory, though I always had the feeling he was the same in defeat. He always said what he thought.

Afterwards, there was frustration that we hadn't won and Ian Marshall was quite upset that he had failed to recover in time to play. There was a sense of anti-climax, having gone that far and played the likes of Manchester United and beaten First Division teams like Arsenal, Aston Villa, Everton and Southampton all in one season, and beaten West Ham so comprehensively. We were punctured. The air was coming out and it was hard to get going again for our final four league games in the week after Wembley, though we were unbeaten in them. No matter how much I told the players we had had a fantastic season and we still had the chance to make it a better one by making the play-offs, they didn't want to hear it. They simply wanted to fade away and do whatever they do. I could sense they were all low.

Before we began the final week of the season, we were given a civic reception on the Monday and I said we wanted to be back again on this balcony, which we were 12 months later after winning promotion back to the First Division after an absence of 68 years. It wasn't simply the fans who turned out that night after Wembley but the town as a whole. Everywhere we went on the open-top bus, we were seeing somebody we knew. The reaction was great and the town had enjoyed it. The feeling was that we had lost, but they had still had a great time.

The players cared, though, and stayed unbeaten in those last four games. We won two and drew two, but we needed to win all four if we were to qualify for the play-offs and we missed out on a top-six spot by three points. Had we made the play-offs, however, we would have been running on empty. We beat Oxford 4-1 in front of over 12,000 two days after playing at Wembley, and two days after that there were over 17,000 at Boundary Park for the visit of Wolves which was phenomenal. The 1-1 draw effectively ended our play-off chances. I will never forget the silence after they equalised late on as we knew then it was going to be hard and we would have to win and rely on other teams losing.

Even after that disappointment, we won at Sunderland two days later and our performance was terrific. Then, two days later, we played at Bradford and drew 1-1. I was invited to a dinner at the end of the season in London where I was given a special award. Brian Moore, the distinguished late commentator, was talking about

the season and how, in those cold winter nights, a team from an industrial town in Lancashire had come along and warmed the hearts of many fans in the game. It brought tears to my eyes and there was no doubt at that time we were everyone's second favourite team.

Unfortunately, the scouts were gathering and we knew we would lose Denis Irwin as Alex Ferguson told me

DENIS THE MENACE......Irwin was immaculate as he attracted regular scouting visits from Old Trafford.

he had had him watched 24 times throughout the season and hadn't received a bad report. We knew there would be changes because we also lost Mike Milligan to Everton and we started at 25-1 to win the Second Division the following season, which I thought was outrageous. At that time, you could insure against promotion bonuses and I told the board of directors they had to do so because we were still a force with most of our players – the likes of Marshall, Barrett, Warhurst, Neil Redfearn, Ritchie and Bunn – remaining. We also signed Richard Jobson after Andy Holden was injured again.

The 'pinch-me season' was followed by a 'keeping the dream alive' one. In 1990/91, we won promotion by finishing as Second Division champions. I still maintain, without wishing to be conceited, that the three years we spent in the First Division/Premier League is one of the modern-day miracles of football bearing in mind we never had proper facilities to prepare on. We had a little training pitch which some wag had christened 'Little Wembley' long before I arrived and it was awful. The surface was full of holes, which appeared like exploded mines. I also used to go in regularly on a Sunday and chase off kids who had squeezed through the bars to play on it.

We achieved what we did without a training pitch and it was something we never got right during my 12 years as manager. We used the British Aerospace sports ground at the Lancaster Club and often we would telephone local schools to use their playing fields. Every day was a challenge, simply to find somewhere to train as any rain left 'Little Wembley' like a bog. Against that background, the achievements of the players were phenomenal because you spend more time on the training ground than on the pitch itself.

We weren't finished with miracles. In the inaugural season of the Premier League came the great escape when we won our last three games in seven days against Aston Villa, who could still have won the title, Liverpool and Southampton to stay up on goal difference ahead of Crystal Palace. We talk about the 'pinch-me season', but really it should be the 'pinch-me five years' as they were crammed with enough drama, thrills and spills to last a lifetime. And even the season when we were relegated, we still went to Wembley for the semi-finals of the FA Cup.

For me, those five years are right up there alongside helping Everton to stay up after they had only eight points from a third of the season when I arrived. We ended up with 50 points and subsequently won the FA Cup and Community Shield. I also won promotion two years running with Manchester City while Ipswich were third from bottom and went into administration shortly after I arrived, yet we finished one

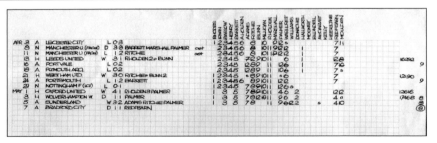

COMMENTARY BOX ESSENTIALS ....the notes and playing records used as reference by Clive Tyldesley during the 'pinch-me season.'

place outside the Championship play-offs despite not being able to do any transfer deals. The following two seasons, we made the play-offs while selling a whole team of players and playing with free-transfer signings and kids.

I have been fortunate in that wherever I have been, there have been highlights. I am proud of my CV. And when you look at the hard times in my early days at Oldham, when we had a visit from bailiffs on the first day of training after I was appointed manager, it made the successes even sweeter. In those early years, it was also about raising the profile of the team. I was often out four or five nights a week pushing over piles of pennies in pubs and attending more darts league presentations than anyone in the country!

And it also showed how tight money was that I would watch Sunday League football in Oldham looking for players and we used to have a triallist in the reserves for nearly every match. We had only 16 or 17 players and during my first year as manager and coach, I even bought towels for training. I didn't realise at the time they had semi-naked women on them, but they were catalogue surplus, hard-wearing and saw us through the season.

We didn't have any weights, so I bought some from a friend who was changing the equipment at his gym. They were the most antiquated weights you will ever see, but we didn't have any so they were welcome. I cleaned the dressing room floor, scrubbed the treatment room with youth-team coach Bill Urmson one day and even marked the numbers of the shirts and still have the stencil kit. It was all a shock from being a player and having everything done for me, to becoming the youngest manager in the league at the age of 32. That puts into context what we achieved.

Littlewoods Cup round by round

Tuesday, September 19th, 1989
Second Round, First Leg
Latics 2 (Ritchie, Palmer), Leeds United 1 (Strachan)

Cup hopes on knife-edge

Latics' hopes of defeating Leeds for a third time in four seasons in the League Cup rested on a knife-edge following their one-goal victory at Boundary Park. It set up a fascinating return at Elland Road, where Latics were expecting to have to withstand a fierce physical bombardment from Howard Wilkinson's new-look team following a multi-million pound rebuild. Leeds were described as having a Wimbledon-style combination of strength,aggression and organisation which hardly made them the prettiest team to watch, although they were highly effective.

Latics endured a frustrating opening in which Leeds stifled their attempts to get the ball down on the ground and play football. Leeds then broke the monotony by taking a 27th-minute lead through Gordon Strachan, the former Manchester United and Scotland star. Latics refused to buckle or be intimidated and hit back with two smartly-taken goals before the break from Andy Ritchie and Rick Holden. Ritchie hammered a cracking right-foot volley past 'keeper Mervyn Day while Holden gave Latics the lead with a bizarre strike. Holden evaded a number of challenges on a weaving run towards goal, only to be tripped inside the box by Noel Blake. Stumbling forward, Holden somehow managed to snake out his right foot to flick the ball past Day for his fourth goal since his transfer the previous month from Watford.

Leeds were stunned and Ritchie ought to have added a third goal before the break, but headed narrowly wide. Latics could have scored further goals in the second half, but Leeds also had chances in what turned out to be a fascinating match of contrasting styles. Bob Young, from the Oldham Evening Chronicle, remained upbeat that Latics could triumph over the two legs. "If they show the same spirit and resolution – as typified by the outstanding Barrett – then that could be enough to book a place in the third round," he observed.

LATICS: Rhodes, Irwin, Barlow, Henry, Marshall, Barrett, Palmer, Ritchie, Bunn, Milligan, R Holden. Subs (not used): Williams, Warhurst.
LEEDS: Day, Sterland, Whitlow, Jones, Fairclough (Blake 38), Haddock, Strachan, Batty, Baird, Davison (Williams 47), Hendrie.
Referee: Mr R Hart (Darlington).
Attendance: 8,415.

<<<<>>>>

Tuesday, October 3rd, 1989
Second Round, Second Leg
Leeds United 1 (Fairclough), Latics 2 (Bunn, Ritchie)
(Latics won 4-2 on aggregate)

Rivals rocked in re-match

Leeds fans were left bewildered as Latics triumphed at Elland Road to march into the third round of the cup. "What the hell is going on?" they chanted, and that was before Latics effectively sealed victory with two first-half goals which left them holding a 4-1 aggregate advantage.

There was no way back for Leeds despite their spirited second-half comeback as Latics celebrated a memorable cup victory against their Roses rivals. Leeds complained bitterly that the goals scored by Frank Bunn and Andy Ritchie were offside. Manager Howard Wilkinson also pointed to his side creating 19 clear-cut chances compared to seven from Latics, though it smacked of sour grapes.

Over the two matches, Latics were the superior side and at Elland Road they mixed grit with polish to deservedly claim their place in the third round. Latics goalkeeper Jon Hallworth did not have a shot to make before setting up the opening goal after 36 minutes with a long clearance. As the Leeds defenders rushed upfield, it looked as though Latics had been caught offside.

The linesman's flag remained down, however, and Mike Milligan gave chase to head the ball over the advancing Mervyn Day with Frank Bunn sprinting past defender Peter Haddock to apply the finishing touch. It silenced the home fans, who were stunned again four minutes later when Earl Barrett's through ball sliced open the offside trap again and Ritchie outpaced the hapless Haddock to rifle home a low shot. Latics, 4-1 ahead on aggregate at the break, knew they were home and dry barring a catastrophe in the final 45 minutes. Leeds made two half-time substitutions, taking off Vinny Jones and Noel Blake and bringing on Gary Speed and Chris Fairclough. It was do-or-die and they had to gamble. They put the Latics' goal under siege and were finally rewarded when Fairclough pulled a goal back in the 59th minute, poking home a left-wing cross from David Batty.

The goal stung Latics back into action and they managed to regain their composure as the Leeds comeback petered out. Indeed, in the final half hour, Leeds managed only one further genuine scoring opportunity when Hallworth smothered a 30-yard drive from Mel Sterland. The double against Leeds, one of the favourites for promotion from the Second Division, again proved that Latics were as good as any team in their division on their day. "They must produce that level of performance consistently in the league if they are to establish themselves as genuine promotion contenders," wrote the Oldham Evening Chronicle's Bob Young.

LEEDS: Day, Sterland, Whitlow, Jones (Speed 46), Blake (Fairclough 46), Haddock, Strachan, Batty, Baird, Davison, Williams.
LATICS: Hallworth, Irwin, Barlow, Henry, Warhurst, Barrett, Palmer, Ritchie, Bunn, Milligan, R Holden. Subs (not used): Adams, Donachie.
Referee: Mr H King (Merthyr Tydfil).
Attendance: 18,029.

<<<<>>>

Wednesday, October 26th, 1989
Third Round
Latics 7 (Bunn 6, Ritchie), Scarborough 0

Record-breaker Bunn

The television cameras were at Boundary Park to capture the drama as Frank Bunn rewrote the record books with a dramatic six-goal haul on a remarkable night. Never before in the 29-year history of the League Cup had a player found the net so many times in one game, and nobody has matched his total in the 20 years since. And the

HOTTEST SHOT IN TOWN.......Frank Bunn engages in some target practice to celebrate his six goals against Scarborough – still a record in the League Cup.

double hat-trick came from a player who was said by some supporters to be losing his sparkle.

By his own admission, Bunn had made a disappointing start to the season. He had not been helped by missing pre-season through injury, but it was a night on which he certainly made up for lost time. Scarborough may have been two divisions below Latics and Fourth Division minnows, but they had to be treated with respect. In the previous round, they had caused a major upset by defeating Chelsea, who were not the force they are today but, nevertheless, were still a top-flight team. Yet Scarborough were swept aside as Latics powered into the last 16 of the competition for only the second time. It was a one-man demolition job from sharp-shooter Bunn as Latics produced a dazzling display in which they could easily have reached double figures.

Bunn's goals came as follows:

10 minutes: 'Keeper Ian Ironside failed to claim a teasing cross from Rick Holden, enabling Bunn to score with a tap-in.

18 minutes: Neil Adams, replacing the injured Roger Palmer, delivered a perfectly-flighted corner which Bunn headed home at the far post.

20 minutes: Ironside made a fine save to deny Andy Ritchie, and Holden knocked the loose ball back into the box for Bunn to score with a left-foot drive.

35 minutes: Bunn latched on to a slide-rule pass from Mike Milligan to calmly slot the ball low past Ironside.

42 minutes: Goal number five in an amazing opening half came when Adams and Denis Irwin linked to set up Bunn, who swept home a near-post shot.

89 minutes: Bunn, who had a share of the scoring record, claimed it outright with a delicious far-post volley from a left-wing cross by Andy Barlow.

Ritchie was the only other player to force his way on to the score-sheet as he hit the sixth goal early in the second half. Even then there was an assist from Bunn, who flicked on a long clearance from 'keeper Andy Rhodes before Ritchie found the net with a dipping volley from outside the penalty area. Had it not been for the heroics of Ironside, who would later have a spell at Boundary Park, it would have been even more of a rout. Ironside pulled off super stops in the second half to deny Irwin and Holden as Latics were unstoppable on a night which belonged to Bunn. He eclipsed Derek Reeves (Southampton), Alan Wilks (QPR), Bob Latchford (Everton) and Cyrille Regis (Coventry), all of whom netted five times in League Cup ties.

LATICS: Rhodes, Irwin, Barlow, Henry, Warhurst, Barrett, Adams, Ritchie, Bunn, Milligan, R Holden. Subs (unused): Williams, Donachie.

SCARBOROUGH: Ironside, Kamara, Clarke, Short (Olsson 46), Richards, Bennyworth, Brook, Graham, Norris (Saunders 46), Robinson, Russell.
Referee: Mr J Martin (Alton).
Attendance: 7,712.

<<<◇>>>

Wednesday, November 25th, 1989
Fourth Round
Latics 3 (Ritchie 2, Henry), Arsenal 1 (Quinn)

Gunners shot down

Cup upsets don't come much bigger than this one as Second Division Latics claimed the scalp of reigning champions and First Division leaders Arsenal. As Sir Winston Churchill, a famous former Oldham MP, might have said . . . this was their finest hour and a half. It was not so much Latics edging victory, but winning emphatically, with angry Gunners boss George Graham gracious in defeat. "That performance was totally unacceptable from an Arsenal team, but I take nothing away from Oldham," he said. "It would have been an injustice if we had gone in level at half-time and, although their keeper made three great saves early in the second half, there was only one team in it. The plastic pitch is no excuse. We trained on a similar surface for two days. The fact is Oldham were by far the better team."

Latics, despite their hugely impressive 22-match unbeaten home run, were still massive underdogs as they prepared to

'PINCH ME NOT'

HOORAY HENRY......Latics midfield man takes a shot at goal on the magical night mighty Arsenal were brought crashing down at Boundary Park.

host the Gunners in the first match between the two teams for 66 years. This was the third time in four seasons that Latics had been paired with the league champions in the League Cup. The omens certainly weren't good as they were beaten 8-2 on aggregate by Liverpool in 1985/86 and then two years later lost 2-1 at Everton to a late goal from Neil Adams, who would later become a key Latics player during the 'pinch-me season.' You only had to look at the starting line-up at Boundary Park to realise the scale of the challenge confronting Latics.

The Arsenal side had John Lukic in goal, a legendary back four of Lee Dixon, Nigel Winterburn, David O'Leary and Tony Adams, then Michael Thomas, David Rocastle, Kevin Richardson and Siggi Jonsson across the middle, and the lanky pairing of Alan Smith and Niall Quinn providing an aerial threat up front. It was remarked that if Latics were to pull off an upset, they would have to impose themselves and play to their strengths in a slick, passing game.

You could see from the kick-off that Latics were in the mood for a shock. They were not fazed by the big occasion and displayed a steely determination to impose themselves on a side packed with internationals. Arsenal, who had never won at

LITTLEWOODS CUP ROUND BY ROUND

Boundary Park, were not allowed to dwell on the ball. "The yard dogs were back, hunting as a hungry pack and snapping at the heels of the Highbury aristocrats," wrote Bob Young in the Oldham Evening Chronicle. Latics could not have timed their breakthrough better. Thirty seconds into stoppage time in a pulsating opening period, Andy Barlow swung over a superb cross from the left for Andy Ritchie to chest down at the far post and score with a right-foot drive from a narrow angle.

It was no more than Latics deserved. Mike Milligan's deflected cross had been cleared off the line by O'Leary while Latics also appealed for a penalty after a dubious challenge by Adams on Frank Bunn. Nick Henry fired a couple of shots narrowly wide and makeshift striker Ian Marshall and Denis Irwin also went close. The Latics defence was hardly troubled, with keeper Andy Rhodes called into action only once to deal with a cross-cum-shot from Winterburn.

It was a different story at the start of the second half when Arsenal, no doubt having received the hair-drier treatment from Graham, set about restoring pride. Rhodes had to earn his corn, making splendid saves to deny Thomas, Dixon and Quinn. Latics weathered that hairy 10-minute spell before reimposing their authority and doubling the lead mid-way through the half. Henry, a 20-year-old rookie, fired home an unstoppable shot from 30 yards – what a way for the Liverpudlian to score his first senior goal as Latics finally had some breathing space. Ritchie sealed victory in the 74th minute with his second goal of the game, starting the move on the half-way line by spreading a pass to Irwin overlapping on the right. Irwin, who was renowned for his excellent delivery, again supplied a perfect cross for Ritchie, ghosting from deep, to score with a glorious header. "We want seven," roared the jubilant home fans and Latics could easily have matched the total they managed against Scarborough as they failed to take a number of other chances.

The celebrations began on the terraces long before the final whistle as dejected Arsenal supporters headed for home, with most failing to see their late consolation goal, a volley from Quinn whose strike did not detract from a memorable night for Latics which Young described as one of their best in post-war history.

LATICS: Rhodes, Irwin, Barlow, Henry, Barrett, Warhurst, Marshall, Ritchie, Bunn, Milligan, R Holden. Subs (not used): Palmer, Williams.
ARSENAL: Lukic, Dixon, Winterburn, Thomas, O'Leary, Adams, Rocastle, Richardson, Smith, Quinn, Jonsson (Groves 66). Sub (not used): Caesar.
Referee: Mr R Milford (Mid-Glamorgan).
Attendance: 14,924.

'PINCH ME NOT'

Wednesday, January 24th, 1990
Fifth Round
Southampton 2 (Le Tissier 2), Latics 2 (Ritchie 2)

Injury-time drama

They say that every team needs a slice of luck on the journey to Wembley, and Latics certainly enjoyed that at The Dell. This was the night the dream would have died but for a dramatic late strike from Andy Ritchie. Four minutes of stoppage time had been played when Rick Holden fired over a low cross from the left which Ritchie, lurking at the near post, managed to divert past 'keeper Tim Flowers. It silenced the Saints supporters who were already celebrating victory and a semi-final place after Matt Le Tissier had put them back in front with an 85th-minute penalty.

Latics, having never progressed this far before in the competition, displayed a never-say-die resolve which was rewarded in the dying seconds of yet another pulsating cup-tie. And even after Ritchie's last-gasp goal there was further agony as referee Roger Milford played almost two further minutes of overtime. But Latics again showed the courage and quality they had exhibited in overcoming Leeds home and away, Scarborough and league champions Arsenal en route to the last eight. Saints, highly placed in the First Division, also discovered that Latics didn't simply rely on their artificial pitch to create a favourable impression.

Latics allowed Saints only one shot on target in the opening half and that went into the net thanks to a deflection off Earl Barrett as Le Tissier put the home side ahead in the eighth minute. It looked as though Saints would finish off the job early in the second half, but a combination of wayward finishing and excellent goalkeeping from Jon Hallworth kept Latics in the match. He made one stupendous save to deny Paul Rideout.

Latics sent on striker Scott McGarvey for winger Neil Adams to provide added firepower and manager Joe Royle was rewarded for his bold approach 10 minutes from the end when Nick Henry chipped in a ball from the right and Ritchie rose to head past Flowers. Latics' joy turned to despair five minutes later, however, when Barry Horne was felled in the penalty area, Milford pointed to the spot and Le Tissier duly obliged to shoot his side in front once more.

Saints were repeatedly warned by the referee for time-wasting and, deep into stoppage time, they were punished when Ritchie struck for the second time. Although it was only a toe-poke which just eluded Francis Benali's attempted clearance on the line, it was unquestionably the most important of the 18 goals Ritchie had scored up to that stage of the campaign.

Sadly, an estimated 600 Latics fans missed the late drama as they were locked out of a capacity 21,026 crowd, the home club deciding to open part of the terracing at the Archers Road end, originally allocated to Latics, to home fans. Latics had warned Saints to expect 2,000 of their fans – 500 with pre-paid seats and 1,500 pay-on-the-day terrace customers. Instead of having three pens on the terracing, Latics fans ended up being crammed into two and there were complaints of overcrowding as fans feared a repeat of the previous year's Hillsborough tragedy involving Liverpool supporters attending their FA Cup semi-final against Nottingham Forest.

SAINTS: Flowers, Dodd, Benali, Case, Moore, Osman, Le Tissier, Cockerill, Rideout, Horne, Wallace. Subs (not used): Ruddock, Shearer.
LATICS: Hallworth, Barrett, Barlow, Henry, Marshall, Warhurst (Donachie 80), Adams (McGarvey 60), Ritchie, Palmer, Milligan, R Holden.
Referee: Mr R Milford (Mid-Glamorgan).
Attendance: 21,026.

<<<<>>>>

Wednesday, January 31st, 1990
Fifth-Round Replay
Latics 2 (Ritchie, Milligan), Southampton 0

Latics march on

Second Division Latics overcame the top-flight Saints to march into the semi-finals of the Littlewoods Cup on another magical night at Boundary Park. Andy Ritchie's love affair with the competition continued as his early goal set Latics on the road to victory which was sealed by a strike by Mike Milligan. These were heady days for the club, who were rewriting chapters of the club's record books in almost every round. The win against Saints extended the unbeaten home run to 30 matches, which beat the all-time record set in 1923/24. You have to go even further back to 1913 to find the one and only other time that Latics reached the semi-final of a major cup competition.

Thousands of disappointed fans were locked out of the big night, although police commander Chief Supt. John Halliwell was hailed a hero after taking a bold gamble

'PINCH ME NOT'

SHOOTING ON SIGHT......Andy Ritchie has another attempt at goal in the Littlewoods Cup quarter-final victory over Southampton.

to allow Latics and Saints supporters to stand on the same terracing. An estimated 4,000 fans were outside the ground 30 minutes before kick-off when he gave the order to allow Latics fans into the same section as the visitors. And, on a trouble-free night, only one supporter out of a crowd of 18,862 was ejected for unruly behaviour. "It was a calculated gamble and it paid off. I think it is a major step forward for football and an indication that the days of treating supporters like animals may be nearing an end," he explained. Chief Supt. Halliwell was faced with the dilemma, with thousands clamouring to see the game, home areas filled to capacity and the Rochdale Road end – reserved for visitors – only half-full. It was a potentially explosive situation, but Chief Supt. Halliwell had to balance that with the risk of trouble outside. The police chief described the behaviour of the fans as "exemplary" justifying his decision to break rules regarding segregation.

The blustery conditions meant this was by no means a classic compared with previous ties, but that was secondary as Latics won through to the semi-finals. They went ahead after nine minutes when left-back Andy Barlow galloped down the wing and crossed for Ritchie to glance a header in off the upright. It was his 20th goal of a remarkable season and eighth in the Littlewoods Cup, which made him the competition's leading scorer. Latics might have sealed victory shortly before half-time when Ritchie had a goal ruled out as Scott McGarvey was deemed offside. What referee George Courtney had failed to observe was that McGarvey had been thrown to the ground by Neil Ruddock and a penalty ought to have been awarded. Justice was done, however, five minutes after the restart when Latics doubled their advantage. Midfield man Mike Milligan started and finished an excellent move with a finish from close range.

Saints took off defender Jason Dodd and went with three defenders, and Latics had to endure some anxious moments in the latter stages. Paul Rideout twice went close, the second chance blocked on the goalline by Nick Henry as Latics at times rode their luck. But they were determined not to let glory slip through their grasp as they set up an all-Second Division semi-final against West Ham, whom they beat in the league at Upton Park in December.

LATICS: Hallworth, Irwin, Barlow, Henry, Marshall, Barrett, Adams, Ritchie, McGarvey, Milligan, R Holden. Subs (not used): Palmer, Donachie.
SAINTS: Flowers, Dodd (Maddison 68), Benali, Case, Ruddock, Osman, Le Tissier, Cockerill, Rideout, Horne, Wallace (Shearer 20).
Referee: Mr G Courtney (Spennymoor).
Attendance: 18,862.

<<<<>>>>

Wednesday, February 14th, 1990
Semi-Final, First Leg
Latics 6 (Ritchie 2, Adams, Barrett, R Holden, Palmer), West Ham 0

Latics nail Hammers

Forgive the corny cliché, but this was a Valentine's Day massacre as Latics fans could scarcely believe what they witnessed as they watched their side hit West Ham for six. It made the return at Upton Park a foregone conclusion, with Latics assured of a first-ever Wembley appearance unless the Hammers produced one of the most incredible comebacks in football history. Andy Ritchie joked after the victory against

'PINCH ME NOT'

TOP SHOT......Neil Adams fizzes a beauty in off the woodwork to open the scoring in the Littlewoods Cup semi-final first leg at home to West Ham.

Southampton that he did not envisage it being a Valentine's Day massacre. It must have been the only thing he got wrong in a season in which everything he did turned to goals. Latics' demolition of the Hammers also dispelled the notion that semi-finals are supposed to be close-fought, tense affairs and certainly not games in which you play with five forwards.

But it was a night when manager Joe Royle pulled off a tactical masterstroke after West Ham came to shut up shop, employing a defensive sweeper and an ultra-cautious five-man back line. Manager Lou Macari fielded a patched-up side, compromised by the absence of players such as Jimmy Quinn, Trevor Morley, Ian Bishop, Perry Suckling, Colin Foster, Frank McAvennie, Leroy Rosenior and Martin Allen. Fortune favours the brave, as the saying goes, and Royle was rewarded for pushing central defender Ian Marshall forward to play as an extra front man as Latics nailed the Hammers with a superbly-confident display of skilful, attacking football.

The floodgates opened in the 11th minute. Marshall's unexpected presence in attack caused havoc as he played a hand in the opening goal, Neil Adams driving home off the base of the post from outside the penalty area. Latics were bristling with attacking menace and it was no surprise when they doubled their advantage after 19 minutes when Ritchie let fly with a shot from outside the box which took a deflection past keeper Phil Parkes. As the heavens opened, it continued to rain goals and the night was rapidly becoming a damp squib for the Hammers. Defender Earl Barrett poked home a third before the break after forcing his way in between two opponents to convert a knock-down from Roger Palmer. Any hope the Hammers entertained of a second-half comeback were snuffed out 30 seconds after the interval when Rick Holden lashed home a left-foot drive. When West Ham finally abandoned their sweeper system by sending on Alan Devonshire, Latics simply switched Marshall back into defence. That failed to curb their attacking play and they added a fifth in the 69th minute when Marshall flicked on Holden's corner and Roger Palmer poached a goal following a scramble. Fittingly, Ritchie had the last word, adding the sixth with a header from a left-wing cross by Holden as he darted in front of two defenders.

It took Ritchie's tally in the competition to 10, only two short of Clive Allen's record haul of 12, and overall the Latics hit-man had found the net 24 times during the 'pinch-me season'. It was a particularly proud evening for Royle, who declared:

GHOSTBUSTER.......Roger Palmer, known as 'The Ghost' because of his elusiveness on the pitch, celebrates his goal against West Ham at Boundary Park.

"We have got to be favourites to make it to Wembley. It was a tremendous night for the town and it would be a great double if the Rugby League club could now make it to Wembley as well."

LATICS: Hallworth, Irwin, Barlow, Henry, Marshall, Barrett, Adams, Ritchie, Palmer, Milligan, R Holden. Subs (not used): McGarvey, Donachie.
WEST HAM: Parkes, Robson, Dicks, Parris, Martin, Gale, Brady, Slater, Strodder (Devonshire 50), Kelly, Keen. Sub (not used): McQueen.
Referee: Mr L Shapter (Torquay).
Attendance: 19,263.

<<<<>>>>

Wednesday, March 7th, 1990
Semi-Final, Second Leg
West Ham United 3 (Martin, Dicks, Kelly), Latics 0
(Latics won 6-3 on aggregate)

Wembley here we come!

'See you at Wembley' was the headline as Latics progressed to the Littlewoods Cup final, the first time they had ever reached the last stage of a major knock-out. The dream finally became a reality, though in essence they had already booked their place in the first leg at Boundary Park three weeks earlier. But, typical of Latics, they didn't do things the easy way and there were some anxious moments as West Ham at one stage threatened to mount the mother of all comebacks. When Latics conceded a third goal midway through the second half and Julian Dicks crashed a drive against the crossbar, there were one or two nagging fears that they might blow what had appeared to be an unassailable advantage. They managed to compose themselves, but it was just as well they had a huge cushion on what turned out to be a nervy night at Upton Park.

Latics had to put up a rearguard action for the 90 minutes and, when referee Terry Holbrook blew the final whistle, there was an overwhelming sense of relief as well as joy. Manager Joe Royle delayed the start of the celebrations in the changing room for 20 minutes as he told the players in no uncertain terms how unhappy he was with their performance. He said: "I am sure we would have done much better in the return had we not had such a big lead. It all fell a bit flat, but we deserved to get to the final over the two legs. It is a great feat for the town, the club and the supporters who have lived too long on bread and water. Now it is champagne and caviar." Captain Mike Milligan summed up the emotions when he said: "We were pretty disappointed with our performance, but delighted to get to Wembley. I think we were complacent and rested on our laurels. We expected it to be hard, but not as tough as that."

West Ham were certainly a different side to the one beaten so comprehensively at Boundary Park. Soon after that defeat, Lou Macari had resigned as manager, with the popular Billy Bonds taking over. The Hammers made light of the fact they had four players cup-tied and Frank McAvennie injured as they set out to restore wounded pride, opting for a three-pronged attack of Leroy Rosenior, Stuart Slater and David Kelly. Latics, for their part, were without Andy Ritchie, who had aggravated a groin strain at Brighton four days earlier. Ritchie had scored in all seven of Latics' matches in the Littlewoods Cup, so there was disappointment that he did not have the chance to extend that remarkable sequence.

Manager Royle was determined to take no chances as he named keeper Andy Rhodes as one of his substitutes in case Jon Hallworth was injured. Latics made a spirited start before the Hammers began to take a stranglehold of the game, Hallworth making a brilliant save to keep out a diving header from Rosenior. Alvin Martin headed the Hammers in front in the 14th minute from a well-rehearsed corner routine. But, when Latics reached half-time with only a one-goal deficit, they appeared to be in complete control. Indeed, the tie ought to have been put beyond the reach of the home side shortly before the break. Ian Marshall waltzed through, but blazed wide with only Ludek Miklosko to beat. The sense of inevitability was to change 90 seconds after the restart when Hallworth tripped Kevin Keen and Dicks scored from the penalty spot to give the home side renewed hope. Marshall could have settled Latics' nerves, but shot wide for a second time after bursting clean through.

And Latics' anxiety increased when Kelly hit the third goal in the 66th minute after he was released by Rosenior's flick-on from Miklosko's long clearance. The first hint of panic crept in and Marshall was pulled back to make a five-man defensive line as West Ham – sensing a sensational comeback might still be on the cards – pushed gant centre-half Alvin Martin up front. Goodness knows what might have happened had they scored a fourth when Dicks struck the crossbar or other chances gone in as Hallworth had to be alert to deny both Rosenior and Keen. As the clock counted down, Latics fans began to celebrate as they realised they would be heading to Wembley to play Nottingham Forest in their first-ever cup final, a historic moment.

WEST HAM: Miklosko, Slater, Dicks, Parris, Martin, Gale, Brady (McQueen 70), Allen, Rosenior, Kelly, Keen. Sub (not used): Dolan.
LATICS: Hallworth, Irwin, Barlow, Henry, Barrett, Warhurst, Adams, Palmer, Marshall, Milligan, R Holden. Subs (not used): Donachie, Rhodes.
Referee: Mr T Holbrook (Wolverhampton).
Attendance: 15,431.

PARTY TIME......Mike Milligan (left), keeper Jon Hallworth and Nick Henry celebrate after the semi-final second leg at Upton Park.

Sunday, April 29th, 1990.
Final at Wembley
Nottingham Forest 1 (Jemson), Latics 0

No fairytale ending

Sadly, there was no fairytale ending to a magical season in which Second Division Latics had captured the hearts of the nation with their giant-killing acts. It was still a never-to-be-forgotten day for the club and their supporters, who pinched themselves to make sure their team were playing in a cup final at Wembley. Nottingham Forest may have lifted the Littlewoods Cup, but it was all about the achievements of little Oldham, who had triumphed against the odds to reach the showpiece occasion.

The club had never been to Wembley before – indeed, the last time they reached a semi-final was 10 years before the home of English football was opened – and the 30,000 supporters who made the pilgrimage to London were determined to savour what was probably a once-in-a-lifetime achievement. Nigel Jemson's 47th-minute goal was all that separated the two teams, even if there was a huge gulf between them in terms of their recent history, success and status. Here were Latics tackling a team who a decade earlier lifted the European Cup for the second successive year. Yet it was one of those days when all that stood between Latics and a piece of silverware was a slice of luck. It was not for the lack of trying as the underdogs, who were without the injured Ian Marshall and Andy Holden and only had Nick Henry declared fit on the morning of the match, gave it their all and did everything in their power to bring the first major knock-out trophy back to the town in the club's 91-year history.

Although it was towards the end of a gruelling season and in sweltering sunshine, you would never have guessed it as Latics pressed forward relentlessly in the style which had become their hallmark. Joe Royle believed the effects of the season had begun to take their toll, but later called for one last push in the final four league matches to try to snatch a play-off place. He said: "We did not play as we can and felt we could have played better. One or two of the players showed the strain as this was our 61st game of the season. We were not caught out on ability, but by a timetable which would even have stretched Liverpool. We have been beaten at the highest level but you have to consider that England international defender Des Walker was named man of the match against a Second Division side."

Forest assistant manager Ronnie Fenton said it was sad there had to be a loser as he praised Latics for the way they stretched his side to the limit and also for their

AXE MEN......Mike Milligan (left) and Andy Ritchie demonstrate the pre-match Wembley message: That they intend to chop down Brian Clough's Forest.

achievements during a memorable campaign. Latics dominated lengthy periods of the first half, but had nothing to show for their considerable efforts. Henry had a shot deflected for a corner while Andy Ritchie's rasping drive was turned over by keeper Steve Sutton as he tried to complete his remarkable run of scoring in every round.

Forest also had their moments and Latics keeper Andy Rhodes had to make splendid first-half saves to deny Garry Parker and Franz Carr. Latics might well have ended the opening period on a high note had Neil Adams hit the target after being released by Mike Milligan. But disaster struck for Latics early in the second half when Forest quickly turned defence into attack and Nigel Clough released Jemson with an astute pass. Rhodes saved the forward's initial shot but could not prevent him knocking the rebound into the net. It turned out to be the only goal – the one with which Forest retained the silverware they had seized when beating Luton the previous spring.

Latics were far from done with, however, as Royle sent on the club's all-time leading scorer Roger Palmer for Frank Bunn to try to inject new impetus. And it so nearly turned out to be a master stroke as Palmer's twisting, looping header looked goalbound until Sutton pulled off a fabulous fingertip save. Latics bombarded Forest for a 15-minute period and a lesser central-defensive partnership than Walker and Steve Chettle would surely have cracked. In their pursuit of an equaliser, Latics were forced to take risks, which left them vulnerable to the counter-attack as Carr and Gary Crosby found extra space. Rhodes made a superb save to keep out a free-kick from Forest skipper Stuart Pearce, but Latics might have snatched a dramatic equaliser at the death when a chance fell to Henry, whose first touch let him down.

There was little doubt that Latics deserved to take the game to extra-time and some argued they might even have snatched victory in the 90 minutes. Not forgetting the fact that this was, against highly respected opponents who, in addition to their European Cup and numerous other conquests, were becoming serial League Cup winners, lifting the trophy in 1978 and 1979, then again in both 1989 and 1990. By beating Latics, they had got their hands on the prize four times overall and so equalled the all-time record set by Liverpool. In addition, Forest had suffered a surprise final defeat against Wolves in 1980 and would also reach Wembley in 1992, when they lost to Manchester United.

Those facts helped underline the uphill task Latics had faced on their big day, though they were well used to seeing the odds stacked heavily against them during their earlier cup exploits. And the Oldham Evening Chronicle's Bob Young summed up the emotion of the occasion perfectly when he wrote: "It was not to be. But, what Latics did, yet again, so amply demonstrates that Oldham has a team fit to grace one of the greatest stages of the world. There were tears of pride as much as disappointment among Latics' 30,000 followers as they gave the players an unforgettable send-off after the match. And, I suspect, there will be more of the same when the town turns out to greet the team on its way to a civic reception. Beaten but not bowed, defeated but not disgraced, they are marvellous ambassadors for the town and for football in general."

'PINCH ME NOT'

FOREST: Sutton, Laws, Pearce, Walker, Chettle, Hodge, Crosby, Parker, Clough, Jemson, Carr. Subs (not used): Wilson, Gaynor.
LATICS: Rhodes, Irwin, Barlow, Henry, Barrett, Warhurst, Adams, Ritchie, Bunn (Palmer 67), Milligan, R Holden. Sub (not used): Williams.
Referee: Mr J Martin (Hampshire).
Attendance: 74,343.

HEROES' HOMECOMING........a shot from the civic reception featuring (from left) Wayne Heseltine, Earl Barrett, Ronnie Evans, Andy Barlow and Ian Liversedge.

Success on a shoestring

Ian Stott, Latics chairman for almost all of Joe Royle's reign as manager, maintains that the achievements of the 1989/90 season were even more remarkable given the financial restraints at Boundary Park. He also believes that it is highly unlikely that a small club from the second tier of English football will ever replicate the success of that incredible campaign. Here, Mr Stott, who was a Latics director for over 25 years, looks back to the glory days of the late eighties and early nineties, as well as the earlier struggles, and tells of the time before the glory days when Royle came close to quitting.

"It would be fair to say that Joe's early days in management were a baptism of fire due to the club's financial troubles. He certainly didn't have it easy. I took over as chairman in 1982, not long after Joe was appointed manager and it is fair to say we owed a lot of money. It was a very difficult time for everybody at the club, Joe included. It was hard and basically we had to sell one player every year to balance the books and that went on for a number of years.

And it didn't come easy on the field as we had some bad runs in Joe's early years as manager, sometimes going two or three months without a win. There was one occasion in 1985/86 when Joe wanted to go. We hadn't won in the league for two months and then lost at home to Leyton Orient in the FA Cup, which was his lowest point. I told him I would not allow him to leave and I would not accept any form of resignation. There was never any question of him being asked to go. He thought things were conspiring against us, but I was convinced it would come good and he was the right man for the job, as it proved by what he achieved afterwards.

It has happened elsewhere in football, most famously with Sir Alex Ferguson, as there were stories that he would have lost his job had Manchester United not won the FA Cup in 1990. The next match after our cup defeat against Orient was at home to Wimbledon, who were quite a fearsome team in those days, but we won 2-1 and

'PINCH ME NOT'

INSPIRATIONAL CHAIRMAN.......a recent photo of Ian Stott, the businessman who helped pull everything together off the field around the time of the 'pinch-me season'.

hardly lost another match, eventually finishing eighth. It was a measure of how bad things were that one of the nastiest things which ever happened to me came on the day we played Wimbledon. As I walked around the pitch from the police control room, I was spat at – the only time it has ever happened to me – and it was not a pleasant experience.

Joe eventually began to stamp his mark on the team and a lot of that was down to his judgement of players. I also have to say that his assistant Willie Donachie had a big part to play as he worked quietly in the background and he was a completely different character to Joe. I suppose the classic was signing Denis Irwin on a free transfer from Leeds. We signed him in May which was an unusual thing for us as you don't want to be paying players in the summer when they are not doing anything. We were so frightened we would lose him to another club that we signed him and paid him throughout the summer before he had even kicked a ball for us.

SUCCESS ON A SHOESTRING

We had a very good run with the Leeds cast-offs, also taking Andy Linighan, Tommy Wright and Andy Ritchie and, had we had a little extra money, we would have signed Scott Sellars as well. There was always an indication that Joe would make a good manager as he had his own ideas and was prepared to stick to his thoughts. I can honestly say that Joe and I got on well. We discussed things at length, but we both had our jobs to do and we didn't interfere with what the other did. While success took longer than anyone thought, including Joe himself, it was always on the cards and eventually came.

Our first success was reaching the Second Division play-offs in 1986/87. Had it been the previous year, we would have gone up automatically for finishing third. I think there was a reaction to the disappointment of losing in the play-offs, as often happens, as we finished 10th and 16th in the next two seasons. I am sure the success of 1989/90 was waiting to happen, although I don't think anybody could have envisaged the scale and magnitude of what we were about to achieve. It was an unbelievable season, reaching the final of the Littlewoods Cup and semi-finals of the FA Cup, and we wondered where it was going to end. I think the 3-3 draw against Manchester United in the semi-final of the FA Cup at Maine Road was the greatest match I have ever seen involving Oldham Athletic. You could not have asked for a better example of a game of cup football. It was absolutely brilliant.

We were unlucky not to win it because Nick Henry had a shot which photographs subsequently showed to have crossed the goalline before it was cleared. It wasn't to be and if you are to beat Manchester United, you must do so first time. There is no way you are going to win second time around as we found to our cost in the FA Cup semi-final of 1994, which we could also have won at the first attempt. On that occasion, Graeme Sharp had a great chance which would have put us 2-0 ahead with a handful of minutes to go, and I think that would have been enough. It took a great goal in the dying seconds from Mark Hughes, possibly the only player on the pitch who could have scored with a volley like that, to force a replay. You cannot take anything away from him, much as I would like to have done, but that was a big disappointment.

Looking back at the Littlewoods Cup run, we began against Leeds. We seemed to play them each season, whether it be in the league, cup or play-offs, and we had our successes. We enjoyed playing them and got on well with their directors and staff. It was good fun because we always knew we would be drawn against them. There were some wonderful games during that Littlewoods Cup run. . . . Frank Bunn scoring six goals against Scarborough, beating league champions Arsenal 3-1, the drama of our equaliser at Southampton in the fourth minute of stoppage time and, obviously, defeating West Ham 6-0 in the first leg of the semi-final at Boundary Park.

There was an aside to the semi-final against West Ham and it was a good thing that we won the first leg so convincingly and were almost certainly through to Wembley. It cost us a lot of money as television had the second leg earmarked for live coverage, but that was changed to Coventry and Nottingham Forest as there was only one goal between the sides after their first leg. It was a case of game on, which wasn't the situation with ours. So, instead of receiving £190,000 – a tremendous amount of money for a live match in those days – we collected only £10,000 for highlights. I was on the Football League's management committee and complained bitterly. And while they did not change the rules that season, television money was subsequently split between the four teams in the semi-finals because it was very unfair how we had lost out.

When you look at the FA Cup run, especially the three games against Everton and two semi-finals against Manchester United, there were some wonderful games of football. United's Bryan Robson would tell you he knew he had been in a match after both of the semi-finals. I had supported Latics from being a boy and was extremely proud that they had reached Wembley for the first time in the club's history. We hadn't been in the top division since 1922/23 and had some lean times in the intervening years, which made this success even sweeter. It has become second nature for some clubs to be wandering out at Wembley, but for us it was a once-in-a-lifetime experience.

There were many who believed that us getting to a cup final was beyond the realms of sensible conjecture. And what made our achievement even greater was that, in those days, clubs turned out their best teams in the League Cup, which is quite different to how they treat the competition today. I have mixed feelings about that because clubs now have such big squads and youngsters coming through that they have to have the opportunity to play on a big stage. Manchester United won it last year, so you can't say they have gone out to a lower-division club in the early rounds.

I felt sorry for our players after we lost in the final to Nottingham Forest as they were out on their feet after playing two, sometimes three, games each week while we were also trying to get into the play-offs. It was an extraordinarily hot day and there were players like Nick Henry, Denis Irwin and Frank Bunn who may not have played under normal circumstances. They were not 100 per cent fit and it was a major disappointment when Ian Marshall declared himself unfit. We were nearing the end of a season in which we played 65 games and the demands were beginning to catch

WEMBLEY, 1990

OLDHAM ATHLETIC v NOTTINGHAM FOREST
LITTLEWOODS CUP FINAL — SUNDAY, APRIL 29

TICKET ARRANGEMENTS

WEDNESDAY, APRIL 11, and THURSDAY, APRIL 12
9 30 a.m. to 7 p.m.

VICE-PRESIDENTS and BOX HOLDERS can purchase their tickets in the VICE-PRESIDENTS' LOUNGE

SEASON TICKET HOLDERS can purchase UP TO THREE TICKETS EACH

from the Main Ticket Office and the Blue Bond Office on production of their Season Ticket and Latics Club Membership Card.

SAT, APRIL 14, 10 a.m.-4 p.m.; TUES, APRIL 17, & WED, APRIL 18, 9 30 a.m.-7 p.m.

LATICS CLUB MEMBERS can purchase UP TO TWO TICKETS EACH on production of their Latics Club Members Card as follows:

£10 SEATS at TURNSTILES 38 and 39 — £25 SEATS at the LOOKERS STAND TICKET OFFICE
£15 SEATS at TURNSTILES 36 and 37 — £28 SEATS at the MAIN TICKET OFFICE
£20 SEATS at TURNSTILES 34 and 35 — £35 SEATS at the BLUE BOND OFFICE

PROGRAMME TOKEN HOLDERS with 10 tokens on a sheet of paper can purchase ONE TICKET EACH on WEDNESDAY, APRIL 18.

**REMAINING TICKETS will go on OPEN SALE from THURSDAY, APRIL 19, during normal office hours.
RESTRICTED TO STRICTLY ONE TICKET PER PERSON**

● Please study the plan below, decide which value of ticket you require, and go to the appropriate selling point ● to purchase your ticket

WELCOME HEADACHES......the reality of having to plan to shift the small matter of 30,000 Littlewoods Cup final tickets from a tiny office.

up on us. Some would say that the number of games we played was ridiculous, but we would not have swapped it for anything, though success brings its own problems.

When I look back, I cannot see a team from our level going so far in the two cup competitions in the same season, even allowing for the fact that many of the top clubs field so-called weakened sides in the League Cup. I think our efforts did fire people's imagination, especially the games against Manchester United, who were taking on the little lads from up the road and receiving as good as they got. I am sure it attracted a lot of interest and there were many who mentioned that they had adopted Latics as their second team after being swept along with the romance of that season. We used to receive letters, even from abroad, in appreciation of what the team was doing, and wishing us well. I would say it was probably the most memorable season in the club's history, though being promoted to the First Division after an absence of 68 years the next year was also a great achievement.

The difference in the three seasons we spent in the First Division and Premier League was that we were playing top-class clubs every week. When you are playing the big clubs every week, you have to be on your mettle, whereas in cup-ties they are one-offs so the seasons were quite different. The last six days of the 1992/93 season were the most extraordinary I have ever known. To avoid relegation, we had to win at Aston Villa, who were second and the only team who could catch Manchester United. We also had to beat Liverpool and Southampton and then rely on Crystal Palace slipping up. They did and we survived on goal difference.

It was a question of how long we could maintain our position at the top level without the resources of the bigger clubs. We had a fantastic run and the people of Oldham enjoyed it. I was honoured to be there and to be part of it. It was a great time in my life and I look back on it with pride. We were lucky that everybody at the club was pulling in the same direction, although, at the end of the day, where you win it is on the pitch and Joe certainly turned up trumps. There is no question about that."

FA Cup round by round

Bunn spares blushes

In a season in which Latics became famed for their giantkilling acts in the cup competitions, they could easily have become victims themselves on a low-key afternoon at St Andrew's. They had to battle from behind to force a replay against the Third Division side and were indebted to a goal from Frank Bunn for the chance to have a second bite of the cherry. Ironically, it was the first time the injury-plagued Bunn – a boyhood Birmingham City fan – had found the net since he scored six against Scarborough in October. The strike against the Blues may not have been spectacular, but it was just as important as his record-breaking exploits in the Littlewoods Cup tie.

The quagmire conditions were far removed from the familiarity and uniformity of the artificial surface at Boundary Park, though Latics acquitted themselves well. And it would have been a travesty had they lost a match in which they were in control for lengthy periods thanks to the commanding form of central defenders Earl Barrett and Ian Marshall. Welshman Martin Thomas was by far the busier of the two keepers as Latics' Jon Hallworth only had one serious save to make – and that in the dying seconds of the game. But it was Birmingham who broke the deadlock early in the second half when Latics failed to clear a deep cross and Nigel Gleghorn scored with a cracking drive.

Manager Joe Royle's response was to push Marshall up front for his muscular presence, leaving only three players at the back. And, sure enough, Latics grabbed

'PINCH ME NOT'

TWIN TOWERS......Latics' appearance against Nottingham Forest in the Littlewoods Cup final was still almost four months away when they embarked on their 1989-90 FA Cup campaign. Could they dare to believe that English football's premier knockout competition might offer them a second route towards Wembley? The two players doing battle here are Des Walker (left) and Frank Bunn.

an equaliser midway through the second half when Denis Irwin set up Bunn, who burst into the penalty area before firing past Thomas. It was not the cleanest of strikes, but fortunately it was good enough to wrong-foot the Birmingham keeper and find his net. The last quarter of the match saw Latics in complete command and they created opportunity after opportunity, but were unable to find a way past the resolute Thomas for a second time and it was Birmingham who were more relieved to hear the final whistle.

BIRMINGHAM: Thomas, Clarkson, Frain, Atkins, Overson, Matthewson, Bell (Hopkins 73), Bailey, Sturridge, Gleghorn, Langley. Sub (not used): Yates.
LATICS: Hallworth, Irwin, Barlow, Henry, Barrett, Marshall, Adams, Palmer, Bunn, Milligan, R Holden. Subs (not used): Williams, Heseltine.
Referee: Mr K Cooper (Pontypridd).
Attendance: 13,131.

Wednesday, January 10th, 1990
Third-Round Replay
Latics 1 (R Holden), Birmingham City 0

Rick to the rescue

In the absence of injured strikers Frank Bunn and Andy Ritchie, it was winger Rick Holden who was the goalscoring hero of Latics' third-round replay victory over Birmingham City. Extra-time was looming large when Holden intervened with a piece of individual magic. He picked up the ball outside the penalty area and evaded three challenges before poking past keeper Martin Thomas – a precious goal that was reminiscent of his winner against Leeds United in the Littlewoods Cup back in September.

It was always going to be a difficult evening without the club's two most recognised marksmen because Latics had a stand-in strike force of Scott McGarvey and Roger Palmer on duty. McGarvey was making only his second appearance in the starting line-up since his summer move from Bristol City, the other being in the much-maligned Zenith Data Systems Cup at Newcastle. Although this turned out to be a tense night, Latics still carved out enough chances to have won by a much more comfortable margin, the opening half remaining goalless thanks to the heroics of Thomas, who pulled off superb saves to keep out long-range efforts from Nick Henry and Denis Irwin.

It remained frustrating following the restart as McGarvey's drive from outside the penalty area struck the underside of the crossbar and, amazingly, stayed out. Latics maintained a stranglehold on the game and were eventually rewarded with 10 minutes left when Holden struck the all-important goal. But it was by no means the end of the drama as Birmingham threw caution to the wind for the time that remained. Latics had to survive some anxious moments and goalkeeper Jon Hallworth made a great stop to deny Simon Sturridge while Denis Bailey poked a shot narrowly wide. Birmingham also had a penalty appeal turned down following a challenge by Holden on Sturridge. This time it was Latics who were the more relieved to hear the final whistle, in contrast to five days earlier when Birmingham were holding on at the death.

LATICS: Hallworth, Irwin, Barlow (Heseltine 76), Henry, Barrett, Marshall, Adams, Palmer, McGarvey, Milligan, R Holden. Sub (not used): Williams.

BIRMINGHAM: Thomas, Clarkson, Frain, Atkins, Overson, Matthewson, Bell (Yates 80), Bailey, Sturridge, Gleghorn, Langley. Sub (not used): Peer.
Referee: Mr K Cooper (Pontypridd).
Attendance: 9,982

<<<◇>>>

Saturday, January 27th, 1990
Fourth Round
Latics 2 (McGarvey, Ritchie), Brighton 1 (Barham)

Manager's masterstroke

Scott McGarvey and Andy Ritchie scored the goals, but it was Ian Marshall who emerged as the key figure for Latics, who reached the fifth round of the FA Cup for only the second time in 11 years. They were facing a shock exit at the hands of their struggling Second Division rivals when Joe Royle produced his masterstroke. The manager went for the now tried-and-trusted switch of Marshall from defensive to attacking duties. And as the Seagulls, with only two wins from their previous 15 matches, discovered to their cost, taking the lead at Boundary Park through Mark Barham's 51st-minute goal was the worst thing which could have happened to them.

Latics again played with three at the back as well as sending on winger Neil Adams for Neil Redfearn as they went for the jugular. And not for the first time in this incredible campaign, the switch was rewarded as Latics mounted a stirring fightback in a throwback to the old days when teams played with five forwards. Adams and Rick Holden began to stretch the visiting defence while Andy Ritchie, Scott McGarvey and Marshall formed the three-pronged attack. Latics were back on level terms midway through the second period when Brighton's Robert Codner failed to cut out a left-wing cross from Holden and McGarvey sneaked behind the defence to score. Two minutes later, they were ahead. Holden was the provider again and Ritchie powered home a header.

Latics certainly had to draw on all their resources after a lethargic opening, no doubt caused by the physical and mental exertions of the Littlewoods Cup draw at Southampton three days earlier. Seagulls 'keeper John Keeley, who would later become a Latics player, pulled off three stunning first-half stops to deny Ritchie (twice) and McGarvey. After he was beaten by McGarvey and Ritchie, he pulled off another magnificent save to keep out a low, left-foot drive from Mike Milligan.

Indeed, without the heroics of their goalkeeper, Brighton would have lost by a far wider margin as Latics maintained their interest in both cup competitions.

LATICS: Hallworth, Irwin, Barlow, Henry, Barrett, Marshall, Redfearn (Adams 61), Ritchie (Palmer 85), McGarvey, Milligan, R Holden.

BRIGHTON: Keeley, Chivers, Chapman, Curbishley, Gatting, Dublin, Nelson, Barham, Bremner (Wood 73), Codner, Wilkins. Sub (not used): Crumplin.

Referee: Mr M Bodenham (Cornwall).

Attendance: 11,034.

SCOURGE OF THE SEAGULLS ....Neil Adams tormented Brighton's defence in the FA Cup.

Saturday, February 17th, 1990
Fifth Round
Latics 2 (Ritchie, Palmer), Everton 2 (Sharp, Cottee)

Comeback kings

Yet another memorable cup tie unfolded as Latics retrieved a two-goal deficit to hold First Division giants Everton to a draw at Boundary Park. Although the Toffees were considered favourites for the replay, the Oldham Evening Chronicle's Bob Young warned that it would be wrong to write Latics off, as was subsequently proved.

'PINCH ME NOT'

SHARP PRACTICE.......Graeme Sharp, who lined up with Everton against Latics and then served at Boundary Park as both a player and manager.

Everton had appeared in four of the previous six FA Cup finals and were a far tougher nut to crack than Second Division West Ham had been three days earlier in the Littlewoods Cup when Latics registered their never-to-be-forgotten 6-0 victory.

Latics, lacking their usual zest, made a steady rather than spectacular start against Royle's former club but created a number of openings. It started to go horribly wrong midway through the opening period, though, when Earl Barrett sliced a clearance to Graeme Sharp, who opened the scoring. Four minutes later, Latics found themselves 2-0 down when Sharp turned provider for Tony Cottee to double Everton's advantage. Manager Royle, aware that a radical rethink was needed, made a bold substitution after half-an-hour, taking off Neil Adams, throwing on Paul Warhurst and pushing Ian Marshall into the attack. Marshall became a nuisance to the Everton defence, though the visitors would surely have sealed victory had Cottee not been denied by a superb save by Jon Hallworth. That was to prove a defining moment in the match as Latics hit back in the final half-hour.

Keeper Neville Southall dived at the feet of Nick Henry and Roger Palmer as he chased a loose ball across the penalty box. He made contact with the latter and referee Tony Ward awarded a penalty which Ritchie converted for his 10th goal in eight matches and 25th for the season. Latics suddenly had their tails up and they struck again six minutes later when Rick Holden's looping left-wing cross was headed home by Palmer for his fourth goal in as many matches. That set up a grandstand finish in which both sides had the ball in the net only for their efforts to be ruled out for infringements. And it was Latics who came closest to snatching victory in the later stages as Palmer, Marshall and Ritchie all went close to finding the net.

LATICS: Hallworth, Irwin, Barlow, Henry, Marshall, Barrett, Adams (Warhurst 30), Ritchie, Palmer, Milligan, R Holden. Sub (not used): Redfearn.
EVERTON: Southall, Snodin, McDonald, Ratcliffe, Watson, Whiteside, Ebbrell, McCall, Sharp, Cottee, Sheedy. Subs (not used): Newell, Keown.
Referee: Mr A Ward (London).
Attendance: 19,320.

<<<<>>>

Wednesday, February 25th, 1990
Fifth-Round Replay
Everton 1 (Sheedy), Latics 1 (Marshall)
(after extra-time)

The late show

Extra-time provided most of the drama and excitement as the tie ended in stalemate for the second time. Latics again more than matched their First Division opponents and took the lead in the first period of overtime with a header by Everton old-boy Ian Marshall which, for 15 minutes, looked to have secured their quarter-final place. It was left to Kevin Sheedy to force a second replay with a penalty which was controversially awarded after Jon Hallworth collided with Graeme Sharp.

The Chronicle's Bob Young described the marathon cup-tie as becoming a war of attrition, declaring that, if it continued much longer, neither side would have enough players. He pointed out that the Latics could be too bruised and battered and too physically drained to pull on a shirt while Everton were in danger of having everyone suspended. Young accused Everton's mean streak of going beyond the bounds of competitiveness and also displaying disturbing petulance. This was underlined, he

'PINCH ME NOT'

SKY HIGH.......Earl Barrett, covered by Ian Marshall, produces a towering defensive leap to clear his lines in the FA Cup fifth-round replay against well-fancied Everton at Goodison Park. It was a sure sign to the Merseysiders that they weren't going to have things their own way against the Second Division upstarts, even on their home pitch.

added, by four Everton players being booked at Boundary Park and five more in the replay when the Toffees also had Norman Whiteside sent off following a waist-high challenge on Mike Milligan.

Young observed that Everton's card count could have been even greater in the two games and he had never seen Latics physio Ian Liversedge called on to the pitch so many times as almost every player needed treatment at some stage. Everton's robust tactics, he believed, were borne out of frustration because, apart from the opening 45 minutes at Boundary Park, Latics had been the better team. In the absence of Andy Ritchie, who had a slight thigh strain, their attack failed to turn possession into clear-cut chances, even when Everton were reduced to 10 men.

Latics had their moments as Andy Barlow forced Neville Southall to make a super save while stand-in striker Marshall had a goal ruled out for a challenge on the keeper before he found the net. Everton twice came close to securing victory in regulation time when Sheedy's free-kick struck a post and the same player was denied by

HAPPY DAYS.....Ian Marshall (right) wheels away in delight following the header to Rick Holden's centre that put Oldham in front ten minutes into extra-time in their replay at Goodison Park. It was a goal that looked like bringing another famous victory against the player's former club – until an equaliser came from the penalty spot.

'PINCH ME NOT'

GOING FOR GOAL.......Ian Marshall again causes all kinds of problems as he bears down on Neville Southall's six-yard area despite a desperate last-ditch challenge. This time, Everton survived – with considerable difficulty.

Hallworth. It was Marshall who made the big breakthrough in the 100th minute, heading home a cross from Rick Holden. Roger Palmer then had the chance to seal victory in the second period of extra-time, but Southall saved smartly from his diving header.

Latics' leg-weary and battle-scarred troops were within five minutes of securing another famous cup triumph when disaster struck, Hallworth conceding the spot-kick which Sheedy converted to set up a third meeting.

EVERTON: Southall, Snodin, McDonald (Nevin 109), Ratcliffe, Watson, Whiteside, Atteveld (Newell 100), McCall, Sharp, Cottee, Sheedy.
LATICS: Hallworth, Irwin, Barlow, Henry (Redfearn 80), Warhurst, Barrett, Adams, Palmer, Marshall, Milligan, R Holden. Sub (not used): McGarvey.
Referee: Mr T Ward (London).
Attendance: 36,663.

Saturday, March 10th, 1990
Fifth-round, Second Replay
Latics 2 (Palmer, Marshall pen), Everton 1 (Cottee)
(after extra-time)

Third time lucky

It was a case of third time lucky for Latics, who finally overcame First Division Everton in a second replay of their fifth-round tie. And it was Ian Marshall who broke the hearts of his former side by blazing a trail to the quarter-finals of the FA Cup for his club for the first time in 77 years. The £100,000 signing from Goodison two years earlier finally settled the marathon with an extra-time penalty which earned a last-eight match-up against Aston Villa after 330 minutes of sweat and toil. Yet again, Marshall, normally a central defender, relished the role of stand-in striker as he had the ball in the net four times, although only once legitimately. And there was no denying that Latics were deserved winners as they claimed yet another top-flight scalp after vice-chairman David Brierley had earlier won the toss of a coin to determine the venue for the second replay.

Once more, victory did not come easily as Latics were forced to battle from behind after conceding a 12th-minute goal scored by Tony Cottee, a cheeky chip over advancing 'keeper Jon Hallworth. They were back on level terms shortly after the half-hour mark when Neil McDonald's awful back pass left Neville Southall stranded and Roger Palmer profited from the error. Latics might even have finished the first half ahead as Neil Adams and Nick Henry both went close. In the second half, Rick Holden's diving header was blocked by Ian Snodin while Denis Irwin's 25-yard drive brought a fine save from Southall, who also denied Neil Redfearn with a smart stop. Everton had their moments as Cottee had the ball in the net twice in the space of 60 seconds, only for both to be ruled out for fouls.

Two minutes of extra-time had been played when the epic tie was finally settled. Marshall was rather needlessly dragged down by McDonald in the penalty area and the makeshift striker gave Southall no chance from the penalty spot. At the other end, Hallworth had to make a fine one-handed save to thwart Cottee as Everton went close to equalising. But, in the second period of extra-time, it was all Latics. Despite the weary limbs they were nursing following all their cup adventures, they were much the stronger side and it was Everton who wilted. Man-of-the-moment Marshall had two clear-cut opportunities, one of which hit the crossbar, while Palmer, Irwin and

'PINCH ME NOT'

MOB RULE......match-winner Ian Marshall is congratulated by delirious Latics supporters following the FA Cup fifth-round second-replay victory over star-studded Everton at Boundary Park.

Redfearn could all have given Latics a more comfortable margin of victory as Everton's last chance of silverware for the season disappeared. Royle's men, already assured of their place in the final of the Littlewoods Cup, were more relaxed, though no less determined and, on the balance of the three meetings, thoroughly deserved their success.

LATICS: Hallworth, Irwin, Barlow, Henry, Redfearn, Barrett, Adams (Warhurst 90), Palmer, Marshall, Milligan, R Holden. Sub (not used): McGarvey.
EVERTON: Southall, Snodin, McDonald (Beagrie 100), Ratcliffe, Keown, Ebbrell, Atteveld (Newell 70), McCall, Sharp, Cottee, Sheedy.
Referee: Mr R Milford (Bristol).
Attendance: 19,346.

Wednesday, March 14th, 1990
Sixth Round
Latics 3 (R Holden, Price og, Redfearn), Aston Villa 0

Villa vanquished

"Put the champagne on ice, we're going to Wembley twice" sang jubilant Latics fans after witnessing another magical night of cup football at Boundary Park.

Joe Royle's men found themselves one step from a Wembley double after claiming the scalp of First Division leaders Aston Villa in the quarter-finals of the FA Cup. There was no denying Latics again as they pulled off yet another upset to secure a semi-final date with Manchester United at Maine Road in this season of dreams. That was the prize for another breathtaking display that dismantled the nation's top team and extended their unbeaten home record to a remarkable 36 games.

It was belated revenge – after 77 years to be precise – for the FA Cup semi-final defeat Latics suffered against Villa, who prevented them from reaching the 1913 final. Villa manager Graham Taylor was gracious in defeat, declaring it was a "red herring" that Latics' successes were attributed to their artificial pitch. He said: "It is the way Oldham play which causes teams problems. They are so direct. They get the ball into the box quickly – more than any First Division team we have met. They'll give any team in the land problems. Every Oldham player knows his job and they play with great confidence. Irrespective of the surface, I am sure they will do well against any team wherever they play. They push up on you, squeeze you, and there is nothing you can do about it. Consistently, they get the ball into areas that hurt you."

Latics had to be patient and it took Rick Holden 38 minutes to make the important breakthrough with a spectacular left-foot drive from outside the box which went in off the underside of the bar. From there, it was noticeable how the self-confidence and belief drained from Villa as Latics stepped up their assault. The lead was doubled five minutes after the restart when Villa defender Chris Price, hounded by Ian Marshall, beat his own 'keeper Nigel Spink with a wayward back pass.

It was all over after an hour when Neil Redfearn sealed victory with his first goal since his £150,000 transfer from Watford. Holden cut in from the left and Spink was only able to parry his shot ,with Redfearn on hand to apply the finish from close range. It could well have been an even wider margin of victory as Roger Palmer, Marshall, Redfearn and Denis Irwin all had chances to add to the tally as Villa were completely outplayed and outclassed. The impossible dream of two Wembley appearances was suddenly anything but that. It was looking increasingly probable while the prospect of promotion still remained very much alive.

LATICS: Hallworth, Irwin, Barlow, Henry, Barrett, Warhurst, Redfearn, Palmer, Marshall, Milligan, R Holden. Subs (not used): Adams, McGarvey.
ASTON VILLA: Spink, Price, Gage, McGrath, Gray, Nielsen, Daley (Birch 58), Platt, Olney, Cowans, Gallagher. Sub (not used): Blake.
Referee: Mr K Hackett (Sheffield).
Attendance: 19,490.

Sunday, April 8th, 1990
Semi-Final at Maine Road
Latics 3 (Barrett, Marshall, Palmer), Manchester United 3 (Robson,
Webb, Wallace)
(after extra-time)

Latics scent Wembley

It is a measure of how memorable Latics' FA Cup semi-final against Manchester United was that it is still talked about to this day. The televised cup clashes on that never-to-be-forgotten Sunday produced two of the finest matches in the knockout's glorious history. And it was very much a day of the underdog as Crystal Palace defeated the mighty Liverpool, who had earlier in the season trounced them 9-0 in the league. The result of that semi caused seismic tremors throughout football, just as little Latics from the Second Division did later in the afternoon when they held mighty Manchester United over an equally-absorbing 120 minutes.

The magnificent spectacle was witnessed by a spellbound 44,026 at Maine Road and television viewers in 26 countries. Manager Joe Royle described it as a great advert for British football while Alex Ferguson referred to Latics as a First Division side playing in the Second Division. Ferguson said: "They are the best side in the Second Division. Newcastle and Sheffield United, who we have played in the FA Cup, are not as good in my opinion. You don't beat the likes of Arsenal, Southampton, Everton and Aston Villa if you are not a good side." Royle also believed his side's performance at Maine Road banished the notion that they could only play on their artificial surface. He explained: "It was nice to hear the spectators singing that we can play on grass. I was aware we had to show a lot of people we can play, but I don't think there is any doubt about that."

Royle was also delighted with the character displayed by his side in twice battling back from behind. It was a tie to savour from the moment Earl Barrett gave Latics an early lead until the drama of 30 minutes extra-time as it had numerous twists and turns. And, while the football may not have been for the connoisseur, the lack of quality was compensated for by the drive and determination, enthusiasm and exuberance of the two teams. While it was battle-hardened United's 18th

F.A. CUP SEMI-FINAL

OLDHAM ATHLETIC

VERSUS

MANCHESTER UNITED

Sunday, 8th April, 1990
Kick-off: 3.30 p.m.
at Maine Road, Manchester.

OFFICIAL MATCHDAY MAGAZINE
£1.00

FA Cup semi-final compared to Latics' second in 77 years, there was no way the boys from Boundary Park were intimidated. They had already claimed a number of First Division scalps in the two cups and simply took this latest encounter in their stride.

They had the temerity to take the lead after only six minutes when United failed to clear a corner. Rick Holden drove in the loose ball, Andy Ritchie distracted keeper Jim Leighton and Barrett stole in to score from close range and send the blue hordes into raptures. United had gambled on including Reds legend Bryan Robson and fellow midfielder Neil Webb, both returning after lengthy injury lay-offs, and the move paid dividends. It was Robson who equalised just short of the half-hour when he was put through on goal by Webb, though keeper Jon Hallworth nearly kept out his low shot. Nick Henry then went close to restoring the lead for Latics, only for Paul Ince to reprieve Alex Ferguson's team by getting back and making a goalline clearance to keep out his shot.

It was United who went ahead for the first time in the 71st minute – and they did so with a scrappy goal. Andy Holden challenged Webb for a high ball and, as

MARSHALL LAW......Ian Marshall gets the better of Manchester United's England defender Gary Pallister to unleash a promising effort in the original semi-final meeting at Maine Road. This one didn't find the target, but Alex Ferguson's defence were still breached three times by the heroic underdogs, who lived to fight another day – and might well have won at the first attempt.

Hallworth came off his line, it hit Webb's head and looped into an empty net. Even then, Latics failed to give up on their dream and were level a mere four minutes later when Ian Marshall found the net with a sweetly-struck volley from Neil Redfearn's cross. On this pulsating semi-final day of goals, twists and riveting excitement, both sides had chances to grab the winner before the match went to extra-time, in which there were further thrills and spills.

Marshall, who could easily have won the game in the closing minutes of normal time, had a shock blocked on the line before United regained the lead when Danny Wallace broke through the Latics defence to score. Latics still refused to concede defeat and, two minutes into the second period of extra-time, equalised again as substitute Roger Palmer ghosted in at the far post to convert a low cross from Marshall. Chadderton's Mark Robins, who only went on from the bench in the second

ROGER RULES......with Jim Leighton floored, Roger Palmer celebrates his goal against Manchester United in the first meeting in the FA Cup semi-final at Maine Road – just part of the drama that spanned two epic ties.

period of extra-time, might then have won it for United while Rick Holden had a great opportunity for Latics late on. In fairness, however, neither team deserved to lose what had been a gripping and highly entertaining cup tie – one that had supporters of both teams longing for more.

LATICS: Hallworth, Irwin, Barlow, Henry (Warhurst 63), Barrett, A Holden, Redfearn, Ritchie (Palmer 95), Marshall, Milligan, R Holden.

UNITED: Leighton, Martin (Robins 105), Gibson, Bruce, Phelan, Pallister, Robson (Wallace 70), Ince, McClair, Hughes, Webb.

Referee: Mr J Worrall (Warrington).

Attendance: 44,026.

<<<◇>>>

Wednesday, April 11th, 1990
Semi-Final Replay at Maine Road
Latics 1 (Ritchie), Manchester United 2 (McClair, Robins)
(after extra-time)

Chirpy Robins ends dream

It was back to Maine Road three days later for the last, gripping chapter of Latics' remarkable FA Cup run. There was more than a shade of irony that the dream of an amazing Wembley double was ruined by an Oldhamer. United's match-winning goal in the second period of extra time came from Mark Robins, who had played football within a goalkick of Latics' ground on Clayton Playing Fields for Boundary Park Juniors. Robins, 20, an extra-time substitute, struck his seventh goal in 10 games, so it was the Reds who booked their Wembley place.

Though Latics lost, they were winners in many ways as their exciting, attacking football had captured the hearts of the nation in what had been a classic tale of David slaying the Goliaths of the football world. Manager Joe Royle was down, but far from downcast, declaring: "It was not to be on the night. We did everything we could do and I am proud of the players. Semi-finals can be cruel and it was a sad ending. I am proud of the players, though. They were superb. We desperately wanted to win this semi-final, but it

has been a lovely adventure." There was also wholesome praise from his opposite number Alex Ferguson, who said: "We have beaten the best team we have played this season – and that includes Liverpool. Oldham are a marvellous team. They are young, quick and have great spirit. They have won all the big games they have played this season and they go into such games believing they cannot be beaten."

It was as though fate had determined that Latics were destined not to make it to Wembley for a second time, though their attempts to reach a second cup final in a matter of weeks could not be faulted. In two splendid matches against United, there was precious little to separate the two teams and it was impossible for any neutral observer to say which was the First Division side. There were many who argued that, with a slice of good fortune, it could well have been Latics heading for a second Wembley appearance. But perhaps it was evident from as early as the seventh minute that it was destined not to be their night.

That is when Nick Henry's shot hit the underside of the crossbar and, to this day, every Latics fan maintains the ball crossed the goalline. There were even calls for

'PINCH ME NOT'

SLIDE RULE.......Roger Palmer lunges in and just fails to make contact with a loose ball under the Maine Road light in the semi-final replay. Keeper Jim Leighton is a relieved man as he just gets there first, watched by skipper Bryan Robson and the latter-day Old Trafford no 2 Mike Phelan.

the introduction of modern technology in those distant days two decades ago. Latics could also point to an incident midway through the second period when Denis Irwin's free kick deflected off the defensive wall and, with keeper Jim Leighton stranded, hit the upright. It proved yet again how slim the margin between success and failure can be.

Both teams created chances in the goalless opening period in which United's Leighton was the busier of the two 'keepers. The loss of Ian Marshall with a thigh strain at half-time was possibly a defining moment of the match as the makeshift striker had been a handful in the opening half and Latics clearly missed his height and deceptive pace. United went ahead five minutes into the second period when Danny Wallace fired in a low cross from the left which Brian McClair finished with a simple tap-in. The Reds were never allowed to feel comfortable with their slender advantage as Latics took off left-back Andy Barlow and sent on Roger Palmer as a fifth forward. And it was a measure of how it unsettled United that Bryan Robson was forced to play as a third centre-half.

Royle tried various other tactical switches as Rick Holden and Neil Adams swapped wings, substitute Paul Warhurst was pulled back into defence and Andy Holden sent upfield. Leighton made a brilliant save to deny Mike Milligan, but Latics achieved the breakthrough 10 minutes from the end. Rick Holden popped up on the right flank and the winger curled an inch-perfect cross for the unmarked Andy Ritchie to fire into the roof of the net from six yards.

There was an early let-off during extra-time when Paul Ince struck an upright, but Latics continued to carve out chances as well as they persisted with their attacking policy when most teams would have settled for a second replay.

Unfortunately, they left gaps at the back and United finally secured victory in the 110th minute. Mike Phelan burst forward on an overlap and slipped a pass to Robins, who managed to steer a shot low past Hallworth. Even then, United were unable to relax as Latics created a couple more chances and the Reds

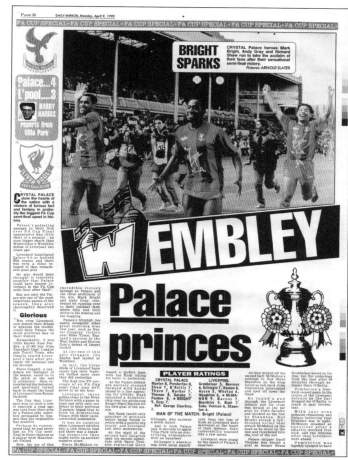

WEMBLEY-BOUND......one team of underdogs made it to the twin towers in spring, 1990, sadly the other didn't. And Crystal Palace's heroes were duly honoured in the press.

were relieved to hear the final whistle – a great tribute to the fighting spirit of Royle's team, who again proved a match for a side costing 10 times more to assemble.

LATICS: Hallworth, Irwin, Barlow (Palmer 57), Henry, Barrett, A Holden, Redfearn, Ritchie, Marshall (Warhurst 46), Milligan, R Holden.
UNITED: Leighton, Ince, Martin (Robins 100), Bruce, Phelan, Pallister, Robson, Webb (Gibson 80), McClair, Hughes, Wallace.
Referee: Mr J Worrall (Warrington).
Attendance: 35,005.

WHAT MIGHT HAVE BEEN.......this big day out proved to be Joe Royle's only Wembley visit with Latics that season.

The players relive their dreams

Record-breaker Bunn

Frank Bunn claimed a place in the League Cup record book with his six-goal haul in the 7-0 demolition of Scarborough, which set up a mouth-watering match against league champions Arsenal in the last 16.

The last thing I thought about when I went out to play against Scarborough was that I would end the night with a place in the competition's record books. It is something I am proud of, together with the fact the record still stands 20 years later. There had been a couple of five-goal hauls, but nothing better than that. And it is nice to be remembered for something which is still referred to on television and in the newspapers. On the night, I didn't have a clue I was in line for a record. All that was in my mind was to take the chances which came my way and to win the game. Of the goals, I would say the sixth was probably the best, not simply because it was the record-breaker, but it was a volley. That made it special.

It is nice that the 1989/90 season is still so fondly remembered. We beat Arsenal, Southampton and West Ham en route to the final of the Littlewoods Cup. In those days, clubs played their strongest teams in the competition which made our achievement even greater. The build-up to the final was incredible and I will never forget walking out at Wembley which was an amazing feeling. Then, when we returned to Oldham, there was an incredible turnout as supporters lined the streets on our way to a civic reception. In the FA Cup, there were some memorable moments as well as we beat Birmingham, Everton and Aston Villa on our way to the semi-finals.

I also scored an important goal against Birmingham, the equaliser in our third-round tie at St Andrews which earned a replay. It was unique for a Second Division team to have two cup runs like that in the same season and we also did well in the league. We would probably have gone up but for our cup exploits, which caught up with us as we had a backlog towards the end. We played 65 games that season and it was tough with so many on the plastic pitch, which was hard to play on. It was like playing on concrete and nothing like the synthetic 3G pitches of today.

Despite the highs of the six goals against Scarborough and the important one against Birmingham, there were also lows on a personal note. I was in and out of the side because of a knee injury and, from what I can remember, I had two or three washouts to try and sort the problem. I missed both semi-finals in the Littlewoods Cup, but was back for the final. In truth, perhaps I should not have played as I wasn't fully fit, but a player is never going to turn down the opportunity to play at Wembley.

When I look back on what we achieved, it was special as we only had a small squad, a unique bunch of misfits which Joe had assembled. There were the likes of Denis Irwin, who had been handed a free transfer by Leeds, and Paul Warhurst and Earl Barrett, who cost £10,000 and £30,000 respectively from Manchester City. We all came together and everything just clicked into place which was all credit to Joe and his scouting staff. I live in Oldham and everyone still talks about that season to this day, and rightly so. It is one of those things which might only happen once in a lifetime.

Goals galore for 'Stitch'

Latics legend Andy Ritchie had plenty to cheer after contributing 10 goals in the run to the final of the Littlewoods Cup and 28 in total for the campaign.

What disappointed me was that I failed to score in the final because I had done so in every round in the Littlewoods Cup up to Wembley. To have got a goal in the final would have topped things off personally for me and may be helped us to win as we didn't deserve to lose that day. Wembley was a tremendous occasion and, together with winning promotion the next season, were the pinnacles of my career. I lived in Shaw, as I still do, and was therefore able to see the impact the cup successes had on the town. When you went out, it was blue and white in the shops.It was great to see how it fired the imagination of everybody in the town and they would all come up to me to wish me well.

The day of the final itself was something I shall never forget, especially our journey to Wembley. It was fantastic travelling on the coach and seeing the

THE PLAYERS RELIVE THEIR DREAMS

FLYING HIGH....Nottingham Forest keeper Steve Sutton makes a spectacular save to deny Latics' Neil Adams in the Wembley sunshine. The winger went as close as anyone to penetrating the defence of Brian Clough's side.

camaraderie of the fans as we passed pubs. And then when we turned into Wembley Way, it was a sea of blue and white and it brought a lump to my throat. I was disappointed for the fans as much as myself that we didn't come back with the cup because that would have been the icing on the cake. Of the 10 goals I scored in the Littlewoods Cup that season, none was more important than the 95th minute equaliser at Southampton that earned us a replay. It was not spectacular, but, in terms of what it meant to the club and what it led to, you could not put a price on it. From what I can remember, Scott McGarvey flicked the ball to Rick Holden and I managed to get on the end of his cross with the ball going in off a defender stood on the line.

There was only just time to kick off again when referee Roger Milford sounded the final whistle – we were as close as that to being knocked out. I know how peeved Southampton were at the amount of stoppage-time played, but we were told by Mr Milford before the game that all the added-on time would be played at the end and we would go off at half-time after 45 minutes. We managed to finish the job at Boundary Park, where I scored our opening goal and set up the second for Mike

Milligan. There were so many great things about the two cup runs that season. We beat so many First Division teams while for me to personally score 10 goals in the Littlewoods Cup was amazing. I was also delighted for my strike partner and big mate Frank Bunn when he scored a record-breaking six goals against Scarborough – something he is proud of. I would pick Frank as the best strike partner I have played alongside as we clicked, both on and off the pitch.

He was the big man who did a lot of the donkey work and took the knocks for me. That allowed me the poetic licence to play and score 28 goals in what was my best-ever season. I was disappointed not to get 30, which I would probably have achieved but for the games I missed through injury. We had such a fantastic team which Joe had got together. There were many who turned up their noses and raised eye brows when he signed some of the players, but they all clicked. And when you look at the 1989/90 season, promotion the following year and three seasons in the First Division/Premier League and another FA Cup semi final, it is no wonder they were called the 'pinch-me years.'

Millie the midfield marvel

Mike Milligan had the proud honour of captaining Latics at Wembley and the young midfield man led the team for most of the season due to the lengthy absence of the injured Andy Holden.

I will never forget leading out the team at Wembley and looking to my side to see Brian Clough and Stuart Pearce and thinking 'Are we really here?' Sadly the day was like Usain Bolt – it flashed by – and I have never known a game pass so quickly. I maintain that anybody playing in a cup final at Wembley should have a week there building up to the game to they can soak up the atmosphere. We were all eager to do well against Forest, but, lo and behold, it didn't happen on the day. We did not perform as we should have done. It had been a great journey to Wembley, which was a momentous occasion, but sadly it did not live up to what had happened before. I am not using this as an excuse, but I had new boots, which only arrived two days prior to the final. I had blisters on my feet in the second half and they obviously did not help

When I look back, my recollections are ones of sheer excitement and thrills throughout the season. It was no fluke that we reached the final of the Littlewoods

Cup and semi-final of the FA Cup as we were beating great teams regularly. And, as our success snowballed, so we grew in confidence. There is no way we felt inferior and we felt we could beat anybody. I remember expecting to beat Manchester United in the FA Cup semi-final. Looking back, we should have gone through to make it a Wembley double.

We had 65 games that season and towards the end of the campaign we seemed to be playing every other day. Manager Joe Royle, who I regard as a second father, and Willie Donachie played a major part in the success as they ensured we had plenty of rest and kept the players motivated, not that we needed to be. What was remarkable was the team bonding, which was phenomenal. There were no prima donnas and we all worked as a team and would help each other out. They were nicest batch of players I have ever worked with and the great beauty was that we all gelled. It was a team full of laughter and, apart from being great players, they all had a great sense of humour. We would work hard, but also play hard. I have never known a group like that one, and that bond still exists 20 years later. Quite a few of us make lengthy journeys to meet up.

Hooray for Henry

Nick Henry was one of the fairytale successes of 1989/90 as Joe Royle has admitted that he was close to releasing the young midfield player the previous season. But a surprise first-team appearance in the Simod Cup at Middlesbrough prompted the Latics manager to have a change of heart.

I remember the game against Middlesbrough at Ayresome Park when I was given my chance in the first team. You need that bit of luck and the breaks to go your way. From that moment, I never looked back. The 1989/90 campaign was my first full one in the first team and I could never have dreamed what would happen. I was so young at the time that I didn't take it in. And it is only now when I look back at some of the games we played that what we achieved that season sinks in. I played in 60 of the 65 games which, looking back, seems incredible. You don't get players today making so many appearances in one season. I played alongside Mike Milligan in the centre of midfield and we complimented each other and clicked from the first time we played together. Millie, who had joined Latics on a free transfer from Manchester City, was already established in the team while I signed as an apprentice at the age of 16. I had

MIDFIELD DYNAMO....Nick Henry, who had a key partnership with Mike Milligan in the engine room of the team.

trained at Liverpool as a youngster, but came to the notice of Latics when they played an amateur side from Liverpool who included me.

It was an amazing experience to find myself playing against First Division teams not long after coming out of the reserves. And, that season, there were so many big games against teams and players I had only previously seen on television and hoped I might play against them one day. Then, suddenly, I was facing them. Beating Arsenal, the reigning First Division champions and current league leaders, set the ball rolling. And it was a dream to score my first senior goal against them in that never-to-be-forgotten 3-1 victory. I remember the ball falling to me outside the box and I managed to get a good, clean strike which flew past keeper John Lukic. That win gave us the confidence and we suddenly feared nobody as we showed by beating a number of other top First Division sides.

When I look at how me and Millie played, we must have been a nightmare for opponents as we didn't give teams one minute's peace. Our job was to win the ball and to play it out wide for Neil Adams and Rick Holden to provide crosses for Andy Ritchie and Frank Bunn. I am sure opponents were beaten before the game kicked off because of the plastic pitch. We had a team who could play on it and we had it worked out to a tee, which was an advantage. What people tended to forget was that we had to adjust our game every other week as we were alternating between plastic and grass. We needed different footwear for the different surfaces.

On the plastic, you had to pass to feet whereas it was a different game on grass so we had to adjust our game each week. It was a remarkable time and certainly a 'pinch-me season,' in which we all went along for the ride.

Palmer the ghost

Roger Palmer, Latics' 156-goal all-time leading scorer, played a pivotal role in the successes of 1989/90, scoring 20 goals, mainly from midfield. He remains as elusive as during his playing days, when he was known as 'The Ghost'. Tracking him down for this rare interview was quite a feat.

I scored 20 goals that season, which equalled my best-ever total for Latics. After a quiet start, everything clicked into gear in the second half, when I scored 15. And there were a number of important strikes in both cup competitions en route to the final of the Littlewoods Cup and semi-finals of the FA Cup. I will never forget the semi-final of the Littlewoods Cup when we beat West Ham 6-0 at Boundary Park in the opening leg, when I was lucky enough to get one of our goals. You never expect to win a semi-final by such a margin and turn the return into a formality. We knew we were already at Wembley. One of the most important goals was the equaliser I scored in extra-time to make it 3-3 in the FA Cup semi-final against Manchester United at Maine Road. I was a ball boy at Old Trafford when I was at primary school, so it was special to score against them, though, by that time, I had more of a leaning towards City, having been a schoolboy with them from the age of 11 before becoming an apprentice and professional.

The only other goal of more importance came for City in the derby against United, when I scored an equaliser in the last minute to make it 2-2. When I joined Latics from City in 1979, they were an average Second Division side with low crowds. We would often be battling relegation and I had no inkling of the success I would later enjoy, though it happened some years after Joe Royle's arrival. We had so many big cup-ties that season and it was amazing how we would regularly beat First Division teams in both cup competitions. Oldham isn't a big place and what we achieved in 1989/90 had an amazing effect as it brought the whole town together. On a personal note, playing in the final of the Littlewoods Cup was the highlight of my playing career.

Not many Second Division teams get to a major cup final and what we achieved that season was incredible bearing in mind the size of the club and their support. I also found it amazing the amount of attention we attracted that season, which is something I had not experienced before. When Latics were an ordinary Second Division side and often near the bottom and battling relegation, nobody wanted to

know us. When we did well, however, everybody jumped on the bandwagon and we were always in the news. The 1989/90 season will always bring back special memories as will earlier breaking the club's scoring record. I don't really go for records and wasn't aware I was on course to become the club's all-time leading scorer until shortly before I broke it. I think the record had stood about 35 years and it hasn't been bettered in more than 20 years since. And, when you look at football today and the way players are continually moving on, it could well be a record which lasts forever.

ROGER PALMER......Latics' record goalscorer.

Final hurrah for Irwin

The 'pinch-me season' was Denis Irwin's last at Boundary Park before he moved to Manchester United and went on to win seven Premier League titles, three FA Cups, the League Cup, Champions League and European Cup-Winners Cup, as well as helping the Republic of Ireland reach the last 16 in the finals of the 1994 World Cup.

I could never have imagined the success we achieved in my final season at Boundary Park. It was amazing to be challenging for honours on three fronts in the Littlewoods Cup, FA Cup and the league. Obviously, the Littlewoods Cup final was the highlight, even though we lost to Nottingham Forest. It was my first appearance at Wembley and I was determined to enjoy the day because you never know whether you will ever go back. Luckily, I did many times, but I did not know that at the time. The two FA Cup semi-finals against Manchester United were memorable and we also had many other great cup matches. It is hard to believe we played 65 games that season and I think I played in 60 of them. That would be impossible today given the pace of the game. It was my last season with Latics because I had decided to let my contract run out as I wanted to try and move onwards and upwards.

And I was lucky Manchester United came in for me that summer. I suppose the success we achieved that season helped as it raised the profiles of both the club and me. When I look back on my career, I reckon there were two huge seasons, and this was one of them. The other was 1986/87 when I arrived on a free transfer from Leeds and did not know how things would work out. Joe Royle and Willie Donachie were huge influences on my career. Willie was also a full-back who was coming to the end of his playing days and looking to concentrate more on coaching. Willie was a great person to learn off and he was also very forward-thinking, as we saw later. Joe and Willie picked me up and dusted me down after I was released by Leeds, and I owe so much to the faith they had in me. The four years I spent playing on the plastic pitch also suited my game as we liked to get the ball forward quickly to Frank Bunn and Andy Ritchie while Roger Palmer was usually on the right in front of me. What also struck me about our team was the sense of togetherness. We worked hard in training but also enjoyed ourselves off the pitch, which you were able to do in that era. I think it is a measure of how close we were that many of us are still in contact with one another and that is more so than with my former team-mates at Manchester United. We were a young team who were getting better and very much on the up. The experience of that season helped the following year when the team won promotion to the First Division as it was known then.

On a wing and a prayer

Neil Adams was signed from Everton for £100,000 in the summer of 1989 and it was his arrival, and that of fellow winger Rick Holden, which improved the service to the front players. One of Adams' enduring memories is the team spirit of the Latics players.

I remember talking to Tony Adams about the group of Arsenal players, which

'PINCH ME NOT'

included the likes of Steve Bould, Nigel Winterburn, Ray Parlour and himself, hitting the national headlines for going out every Tuesday night. I can tell you that we invented the 'Tuesday Club' long before Arsenal – and Joe Royle was happy for us to go out as Wednesday was our day off. Whereas four or five Arsenal players would go out, we would have 13/14 in our group and it is rare to have such a great team spirit at a club. It was that sense of togetherness that played a big part in our success. It wouldn't happen today because of the way the game has gone, but it was not frowned upon in those days. I spent two months on loan from Everton earlier that year and Joe Royle came in for me in the summer, along with Allan Clarke at Barnsley, while a top-flight club also showed interest.

Everton had also offered me a new contract, but, after Howard Kendall left, my chances dwindled with Colin Harvey in charge. I felt I had the choice of a couple of years mainly in the reserves or playing regular first-team football, which I needed. I decided to join Latics because I had the advantage of having been there and seen the potential. It may, on the face of it, have appeared that I had gone from one of the best teams in Europe, as Everton were, to a struggling Second Division team, but I knew I was joining a good team who had not been punching their weight. That was proved when everything clicked. It was unbelievable how we went from being 16th in the Second Division to reaching the final of the Littlewoods Cup, semi-finals of the FA Cup and narrowly missing out on promotion in the space of 12 months.

That season also proved we were more than capable of playing at a higher level than the Second Division. And the way things took off that season, when we were regularly beating top First Division teams, it certainly made everyone in the country sit up and take note of what we had achieved. There were so many big games, but the one which stands out was the 6-0 victory against West Ham at Boundary Park in the Littlewoods Cup. You don't expect scores like that in semi-finals. It was one of those magical nights under the lights. The place was packed to the rafters and rocking. West Ham were expected to beat us over the two legs, but we ripped them to shreds and to win the way we did was incredible. I scored the first, so I maintain that it was my goal which got us to Wembley. But for a catastrophe in the second leg, we knew we were in the final and we had put little Oldham on the map.

It had been an amazing run from Frank Bunn scoring six against Scarborough to us beating First Division champions Arsenal and Southampton, another top-flight team. Obviously, the plastic pitch was a big advantage as we knew how to play on that surface by passing to feet. When we won promotion the next season, and the artificial surface was replaced by grass, there were people saying the plastic boys would go down without winning a game. It was pleasing, therefore, that we survived comfortably in our first season in the First Division and see them having to eat their words. I am often asked why we had such a special side. Apart from the team spirit, Joe bought well, as was later proved when the likes of Denis Irwin, Earl Barrett, Paul Warhurst and Mike Milligan went on to play at the highest level. He liked to play with two wingers and that summer brought in Rick Holden and me to provide service for Andy Ritchie, Frank Bunn, Roger Palmer and Ian Marshall – and we easily slotted into the team.

Heartbreak for Holden

Andy Holden suffered the heartbreak of missing a Wembley appearance after being injured at Portsmouth five days before the final of the Littlewoods Cup. It provided further misery for the club captain, who had only recently returned to action following a seven-month lay-off through damaged ankle ligaments.

I strained my hamstring on a heavy pitch at Portsmouth days before the final of the Littlewoods Cup, which was horrendous, heartbreaking and gut-wrenching. You don't often get chances like that in your career, so I was desperate to play and, while I was delighted for the boys, it was awful for me. As club captain, I remember going into the dressing room afterwards and saying how proud I was of the lads who had done brilliantly. I used to say Oldham was the coldest place on the planet, but, during that season, it was the hottest. It was a great place to be, we had a fantastic team and the place was alive and buzzing during the two great cup runs. I was injured three games into the season and only returned in time to play in the FA Cup semi-final. There were worries about me lasting the game as I had only played a couple of matches leading up to the game against Manchester United. I played both the semi-final and replay and there was a fantastic atmosphere at Maine Road each time.

I was up against Mark Hughes and knew 'Sparky' from the time we had played together for Wales. We had two ding-dong battles in the semi-finals. In the first game, he gave me a thick lip and he had a black eye. When we locked horns again on the Wednesday, he elbowed me on the nose. He was a tough nut to crack. In the replay, Joe pushed me up front towards the end to try and get a knock down and ruffle feathers for our strikers, who were up against Steve Bruce and Gary Pallister. We had a great team when you look at the likes of Denis Irwin, Andy Barlow, Earl Barrett

Paul Warhurst

One of the more pleasing bonuses of the Latics' huge successes of the past 18 months has been the manner in which several of the club's players have been thrown into the international spotlight.

Last season Dennis Irwin and Mike Milligan were both introduced to the Republic of Ireland under-21 side and, since then, Dennis has gone on to collect two full caps.

The latest player to win recognition is Paul Warhurst whose performances over the past year earned him a richly deserved chance in the England under-21 side.

Paul made his debut in the 3-1 victory over Hungary in September. A solid performance that day earned him another chance in the UEFA Under-21 Championshp tie against Poland a month later. England lost that game 0-1 but Paul was back in the side again for the goalless draw with Wales early this month.

Paul has time very much on his side so there is every chance that he will one day play for the full England team.

Manchester City signed Paul as a trainee in July 1986 and, after he had progressed well in their youth and reserve teams, he was offered a professional contract in July 1988.

City at the time had a large batch of promising young players coming through to their senior side but Paul was not at Maine Road long enough for his League opportunity to come around.

He was transferred to the Latics in October 1988, making his debut in our Second Division side at Portsmouth that same month. He made occasional subsequent appearances during the course of that season and in January 1989, when we were savaged by a series of injuries to our strikers. Paul played in the unusual position, for him, as striker at Charlton in the third round of the F.A. Cup.

The Latics took an early lead at Selhurst Park that day and, though Charlton rapidly equalised, we seemed to be heading for a certain replay until the home side snatched victory in injury time.

But, if we lost out on Cup glory that season, Paul certainly made up for it last term as the Latics progressed to the semi-finals of the F.A. Cup and the final of the Littlewoods Cup.

Paul appeared as substitute in both semi-final games with Manchester United but he was voted as one of our star performers at Wembley as we lost so narrowly to Nottingham Forest.

This season England's new assistant-manager Lawrie McMenemy, who had been highly impressed with his Wembley performance, took time out to watch Paul again. He liked what he saw and, as a result, Paul got his chance in the England under-21 side in September.

and Paul Warhurst at the back, dual-purpose player Ian Marshall, Jon Hallworth and Andy Rhodes (who alternated as goalkeepers), the two ratters (Milligan and Henry) in the centre of midfield, wingers Rick Holden and Neil Adams, and then Andy Ritchie, Frank Bunn and Roger Palmer up front. I used to room with Roger, who was a great character and my best mate.

When I signed for Latics for a club-record fee in January, 1989, the team were having a terrible time. We had a crisis meeting and Joe told us we would be running for a week. We ran in threes and I had Earl on one shoulder and Roger on the other. Before I put a foot forward, they had sprinted 30 yards clear of me. Everybody says Brian Clough and Matt Busby were managers ahead of their time, but the same applies to Joe, who was a very clever manager as well as being a lovely man. His man management was second to none and the players would run through brick walls for him.

Marshall's front-line move

Ian Marshall proved to be Joe Royle's secret attacking weapon during the 1989/90 season as the Latics manager would regularly switch him from the centre of defence to the front line in pursuit of a goal when things weren't going to plan on the field.

It was during our promotion campaign the following season that I became more of a permanent striker. I started my career as a centre-half and that is the position I was signed to play for Latics when I moved from Everton in 1988. The reason I was switched to become a striker – something which began in the 'pinch-me season' – was because I kept pestering Joe to play me up front. My fall-out with him over where I played in the team has been well documented. I wanted to play up front while he has gone on record as saying that had I stayed as a centre-half, he could have seen me playing for England. But if a player scores a goal, the feeling far outweighs any other and is better than making 10 goalline clearances or 20 last-ditch tackles.

Had I only ever played as a centre-half, I would have been satisfied. But once I had played up front and scored goals, it was always in my mind to stay there. I have some brilliant memories, especially the FA Cup semi-final against Manchester United when Joe gave me a starting spot up front, which was rare at that time. It still ranks as possibly the best semi-final day in the history of the competition. I remember watching Crystal Palace causing a massive upset by beating Liverpool 4-3 in the hotel and thinking we had to follow that. I thought our match would, by contrast, probably be a dour goalless draw. It was anything but that as it finished 3-3 after extra time.

Obviously, the three games against my former club Everton in the fifth round of the FA Cup were memorable. In the first at Boundary Park, we came back from 2-0 down. When Roger Palmer made it 2-2, I ran into the net behind which the Everton fans were and gave them a v-sign. I would have been banned for doing that. It was great to score in the replay at Goodison Park and, for a short time, it looked like being the match-winning goal. But one of the highlights of that season was scoring the penalty which earned us victory against Everton in the second replay at Boundary Park. I celebrated with twisted joy, just like Maradona did when he scored for Argentina and ran towards the television cameras – a shot which is still shown today on television.

In one of the games against Everton, I was punched – I cannot remember by whom – and my nose was flattened. I was black and blue when I was interviewed afterwards on television. After those highs came the massive low of missing the final of the Littlewoods Cup through injury. I picked up a niggling thigh strain in the FA Cup semi-final replay and didn't play again that season. I had a fitness test on the morning of the final and obviously was very, very disappointed when I failed and knew I could not play. When I got to Wembley I went to the players' lounge where Neil Kinnock, a great icon of the day and my father's hero, was. I spent the afternoon drinking with him and I am afraid I was worse for wear by the time the team stopped at Northampton for a meal on the journey home.

I have some fantastic memories of that season and also my five years at Oldham. I am frequently asked about my proudest moment in football and I say it was helping

Latics reach the First Division, today's Premier League. Those things never happened in Oldham, a little mill town, and will probably never do so again. When I arrived at Oldham, I am sure crowds averaged less than 5,000 but, when we got into the First Division/Premier League, they had risen to around 18,500. It must have been paradise for burglars as everybody in the town was at the match on a Saturday afternoon.

Earl the defensive lord

Earl Barrett went on to make a £1.7million move (still a club record) to Aston Villa in 1992 and he also won three full caps for England.

It was as though we were on the crest of a wave and did not put a foot wrong for about two and a half years. The 1989/90 season was incredible as we had two great cup runs and were also challenging for promotion, which was unbelievable. Obviously, the final of the Littlewoods Cup was the highlight while the FA Cup semi-finals also stood out, especially as I scored against Manchester United. From a

personal view, it could not have gone any better as I had solid partnerships in the centre of defence with both Paul Warhurst and Ian Marshall. Maybe it was luck or maybe it was good management from Joe Royle, but we hit it off and, whatever Joe did, seemed to work.

You only have to look at Manchester City this season to see how big-money signings Kolo Toure and Joleon Lescott have struggled to form a partnership at the heart of their defence. Obviously, there were a lot of games for us, but, when you have the momentum in your favour, all you want to do is

EARL'S EXTRA HELPING.....not only was Earl Barrett a class defender. He was also an attacking threat and scored four goals in 1989/90.

keep playing. We didn't want it to end and that season was the highlight of my time with Latics. I often wonder how little Oldham managed it and that it is something which may never happen again.

I had arrived a couple of years earlier from Manchester City, where I was a regular in the reserves. I loved it at City and was scared leaving to move into another environment, but it is something I had to do. I needed to be playing regular first-team football to develop my career and I certainly achieved that with Oldham. In those cup runs, I was able to test myself against some of the top strikers in the game, the likes of Manchester United's Mark Hughes, and I managed to do well against them.

The publicity and air time the club received that season was amazing as little Oldham knocked out yet another First Division team. It was great for me and also other individuals at the club. That was underlined at the end of the season when I received a call up to the England under-21 team. You hear about players turning down the chance to play for the under-21s, which I find incredible. There was not a chance of me doing that, even though it was at the end of a long, hard season and I could have done with the rest. I couldn't wait to join up with the England squad and get the chance to play for my country.

Home sweet home for Andy

Andy Barlow, a left-back who served Latics with distinction for 11 years, had the honour of being the lone Oldhamer in the team. As he explains, that made the achievements of 1989/90 even more special for him.

Every professional footballer dreams of playing at Wembley, so reaching the final of the Littlewoods Cup was the fulfilment of that. But for me to achieve it with my home-town club was extra special and it certainly meant a lot to me. You had the feeling that every person on the terraces had the personal dream, which I was lucky enough to see come true. And reaching the final carried different personal expectations for me because it was the town where I was born. You can imagine how proud I felt walking out at Wembley in front of 30,000 fans from Oldham. The whole town was buzzing that year because of the success we achieved and the football club certainly put Oldham on the map. The publicity of our cup runs generated a lot of business, not only for the football club, but also the town. Suddenly, everybody knew about Oldham Athletic and you were recognised in the street whenever you went.

BARKING ORDERS......Andy Barlow plays the role of organiser as he urges more from his team-mates in the heat of battle.

That was nice, but it eats into your normal life and you could imagine how difficult it is for the big names in football, who are unable to enjoy privacy or anonymity.

They were two amazing years as the next season we won promotion and returned to the First Division after an absence of 68 years. And the second season was the climax of what we had been working to achieve. I am afraid much of the season is now a blur. I wish I could remember more. It is a pity we weren't in the digital age and there was more footage, but I have a couple of videos and two boxes of newspaper cuttings in the attic. They are great to look at.

Curiously, what I remember most is the chaotic finish, in which we played five games in nine days. There was no recovery time and there were times when I could barely walk, though there was nothing we could do about that. We were victims of our own success. We were an exciting team to watch, immense going forward and had some talented individuals. I think we relied on the front players to bail us out because some of our defending was not clever – as I have discovered when watching the videos. What captured the nation's hearts was the fact that we won by playing excellent, attacking football.

Holden haunted by failure

Rick Holden was a late arrival at the party, only signing for Latics from Watford in a surprise £165,000 transfer 48 hours before the kick-off to the new campaign, a move he was not to regret. He does, however, have a controversial take on the 'pinch-me season.'

THE PLAYERS RELIVE THEIR DREAMS

The fans loved the cup runs because they were so unexpected. When I look back, however, I view the season as a failure as we didn't win anything. We didn't even get into the promotion play-offs. I still clearly remember driving home after the last game of the season and thinking what a waste of time it had been as we had not won anything. But it gave us hunger and, when we reported back for the following season, it made us even more determined to get out of the league. I would describe winning promotion as a greater achievement than what happened in 1989/90. I would rather mark that than celebrate defeat, even though we reached the final of the Littlewoods Cup and semi-finals of the FA Cup.

As for my time at Watford, I don't know why things went wrong for me as,

towards the end of the previous season, we ought to have gained automatic promotion. Our manager Steve Harrison started mucking about with the team and I found myself dropped as we failed to even make the play-offs. When I was left out of the team for pre-season matches, I quickly realised the writing was on the wall for me. I went to see Steve on the Monday before the start of the season to put in a transfer request and was told to go home because Joe Royle was going to ring me. That is how the transfer came about. Joe had wanted to sign me when I left Halifax for Watford, but couldn't afford to and monitored me instead.

The previous season had been disappointing for Latics as they finished in the bottom

ON THE RUN.....winger Rick Holden was the scourge of defenders as he rampaged down the left flank.

half of the table. I remember playing against them for Watford at Boundary Park, along with Neil Redfearn, who moved not long after I arrived, and they were poor. I recall asking Redders afterwards how on earth had we lost 3-1. It was in February and Latics were fourth bottom. The victory against us was their first in 12 league matches and it proved to be the turning point of their season, which had become a battle against relegation.

When I joined Latics, I didn't realise how good a team we would become as we had only been an average Second Division side the year before. But it quickly dawned on me that there was enormous talent in the squad. I saw the capabilities and the way we played, and all that was needed was the spark and belief. We had some very good strikers, like Andy Ritchie, Frank Bunn and Roger Palmer, and Ian Marshall when he was pushed up from defence. They needed good early service and Joe had obviously identified that as a priority as he had brought in Neil Adams and me during the summer. They say wingers work in pairs and we worked well together. Joe decided on a plan of action, which was to attack and, to his credit, he let us get on with our jobs.

It was a remarkable season in which nobody expected an average Second Division side to batter First Division teams into submission in both cup competitions. And, as it progressed, we quickly grew in confidence and, as a result of that, the talent in the side shone through. We beat a lot of top First Division teams and that season instilled a belief that, should we be promoted, as we were the following year, we had the quality to survive. We had nothing to fear and we could live with these boys if we played them on a regular basis as we were to prove.

We had some very good players in the squad and you can see most of them went on to have good careers at other clubs and play at the highest level. That was all credit to Joe because the team were made up of odds and sods as he raided the reserve teams of Manchester

MR VERSATILE....Ian Marshall was at home for Latics in both defence and attack.

City and Leeds and got the likes of Ian Marshall and Neil Adams from Everton and myself from Watford. He gave us all the chance to blossom into first-team players. When I look back at the season, it was sad that we ended up empty-handed as the exhaustion caught up with us. We played 65 games with a small squad and, basically, we were all knackered. There was nothing left in the tank. I am convinced that, had we played the final of the Littlewoods Cup in Februsry, when it is staged today, we would have beaten Nottingham Forest.

All Rhodes lead to Wembley

Andy Rhodes was Latics' goalkeeper at Wembley, though he only regained his place in the side two matches before the final of the Littlewoods Cup. He replaced Jon Hallworth, who had been first choice for the preceding three and a half months, having regained his place for the New Year's Day league match at Leeds United.

It must have been a tough call for Joe Royle deciding which keeper to play in the final but, fortunately, it was a good one for me. I had a long run in the side in the opening half of the season, when Jon Hallworth was ruled out through injury. Jon got back into the team and played the majority of games in the second part, including the two FA Cup semi-finals against Manchester United. When you are not in the side, you simply have to get on with things and make sure that, when you get another chance, you are ready to take it.

I had never given up hoping of getting back into the side and playing at Wembley because you cannot afford to have such thoughts. You always have to believe you have a chance of playing. I was lucky enough to have possibly my best game of the season at Wembley, where a few of our lads were carrying injuries which needed operations in the summer. But, having said that, we still had great chances to beat Nottingham Forest. None of us had played there before, so it was emotionally overwhelming and it was terrific for providing me with some rocking chair moments for later in life.

That was one of the highlights of my career, as was later playing for Dunfermline against Hibernian in the final of the Scottish League Cup at Hampden Park. I have been lucky to play in League Cup finals in both England and Scotland. When I look back at 1989/90, I am convinced we should have also won through to the final of the

FA Cup because we more than matched Manchester United over the two matches. And, on another day, things may well have gone our way. The two cup runs were fantastic and we had some magical matches. To beat First Division teams on a regular basis in both competitions was something special. There were so many highlights, but my main one was being in the side who beat Arsenal, the First Division champions and leaders when they visited Boundary Park. There was nothing lucky about our victory and we might even have won more emphatically than 3-1.

The season was one high after another and we were certainly on the crest of a wave. What struck me was the unity of the team, which I am sure helped us to get some of the results we achieved. It was very much a case of us all being in it together as a squad and that sense of togetherness was unique and something which has not happened to me at other clubs I have played for. We are all still friends 20 years on and many of us meet up regularly which is again unusual because, in football, players don't normally keep in such close contact.

Dual role for Donachie

Willie Donachie was Joe Royle's No 2 during the 'pinch-me season' and the lower-profile member of the successful managerial partnership. Preferring to stay in the background and off the radar, Donachie was still playing whenever needed despite being 38 years of age by the end of the campaign. Indeed, he made eight starts in the 1989/90 season.

When I look back to that season and the fantastic times we had, it was down to a lot of hard work from various people at the club over a number of years finally coming together. I have been in football all of my life and have seen that it has to be right at the top for a club to be successful. If things are not right in the boardroom, it is very hard to achieve success. And we were lucky to have a board containing young, ambitious directors, who let me and Joe get on with the job.

There wasn't undue pressure because everybody at the club was aware that for Oldham to get into the First Division would be a miracle, though we achieved that the next season. It was a far cry from when I came to England in the late sixties and Oldham were in the Fourth Division. When Joe and I were later at Ipswich, however, expectations were far different. They were expected to be in the Premier League. I felt at times we did an even better job than at Oldham as we helped Ipswich, despite their financial troubles, reach successive promotion play-offs and yet that was still not good enough. Managing at that level is far removed to what it is like in the top division, where money is no object.

Joe did an unbelievable job at Oldham as he would have to sell his best players to balance the books and then produce an even better team. We regularly used to steal off the likes of Manchester City and Leeds. Indeed, we had an unbelievable time with Leeds, getting Denis Irwin on a free transfer, Andy Linighan, Andy Ritchie and Tommy Wright, while we also captured Earl Barrett and Paul Warhurst from Manchester City. But, for a club like Oldham, it was still a significant gamble even when we signed those players.

We had a lot of good, young players with no big egos and they worked hard. They were in an environment that gave them chance

WILLIE DONACHIE

DUAL ROLE....Willie Donachie served both as a player and as Joe Royle's No 2. The former Scotland international full-back made eight starts during the 'pinch-me season.'

to progress. You only have to look at somebody like Bill Urmson, who gave a massive part of his life to bringing through young players. Things simply came together that season and the cup runs were remarkable as we beat First Division sides round after round and there was a feeling that anything was possible. The only thing which hindered us at the end of the season was the huge number of games we played and it took so much out of the lads. That is why we narrowly missed out on reaching the play-offs.

There were so many highlights that season as we beat First Division champions Arsenal, Southampton, Everton and Aston Villa, who were all top sides, and so nearly got the better of Manchester United in the FA Cup semi-final. They were great times for the Oldham fans, the diehards who had supported the club all their lives and seen little success. They were down-to-earth and warm and, when we got into the Premier League, they never expected us to win it. They were simply happy for their side to be playing top teams every week.

The three years we spent in the First Division/Premier League were also fantastic times for the town. And who will ever forget the 'Great Escape' of 1992/93, when we needed to win our last three matches, and also rely on Crystal Palace slipping up, for us to stay up? We did just that on goal difference and it was as though the Gods were with us that season as Palace threw away their chance and we took ours. I would describe the three years we spent in the top division – and also the season when we were promoted – as an even bigger achievement than the events of 1989/90.

Reserve to regular

Paul Warhurst was in his first full season with Latics following a £10,000 transfer from Manchester City, where he was in his teens and in the reserves as a defender.

It was quite a turnabout in my career going from Manchester City's reserves to playing in the final of the Littlewoods Cup at Wembley in the space of 18 months. It turned out to be a fantastic career move as, not only did I get regular first-team football, but we had great players and enjoyed great success. I have a lot of good memories from 1989/90, especially the FA Cup semi-finals against Manchester United at Maine Road and the Littlewoods Cup final, which was the icing on that marvellous season. I was fortunate to play at Wembley seven or eight

MAN ON THE MOVE.......Paul Warhurst, who underwent changes in more ways than one.

times, but the first time always remains special. I was 20 and the whole experience of being involved in the build-up was fantastic and something I will never forget. I will always remember the coach journey to Wembley and arriving to see a sea of blue and white. And, as for the game, I thought we did well and were unlucky to lose.

What I also remember about that season was that we were blessed with a fantastic bunch of young players. It was an indication as to the talent in the team that so many went on to play at the highest level, including Earl Barrett. He played alongside me in the centre of defence, though I also played at right-back that season. I think one of the reasons why Earl and I did so well was that we both had a lot of pace, which is important to get yourself out of trouble. In those days, Earl was called 'The Rucksack' because he would stick to the back of forwards. I also partnered Ian Marshall in the centre of defence and he was big, gangly and a handful, with a knack of annoying opponents.

I was lucky to play for a team who played football the way it ought to be played. We got the ball down and developed a passing game. The plastic pitch obviously helped as there was no way you could play a long-ball game on that. It encouraged you to play football and brought you on as a player. Joe Royle and Willie Donachie also encouraged us to pass the ball and it was a joy to play football in that team.

Surprise, surprise for Gary

Gary Williams was a peripheral figure in the exploits of 1989/90, though there was to be a fairytale ending for the player who missed a sizeable chunk of the season through injury. He made only two starts, but appeared in a further 25 matches as a substitute.

I didn't expect to be in the squad for the final of the Littlewoods Cup, never mind be named as one of our two substitutes. While it was a great season for the team, it had been a disappointing one for me as I had picked up a succession of injuries. I had a couple of operations on my knees and was only just back from the latest one, so I didn't expect to be involved at Wembley. You can imagine my surprise when I was named in the squad – and the shock when it was announced Roger Palmer and I would be the two substitutes.

My joy was a stark contrast to how goalkeeper Jon Hallworth felt. I lived with Jon at that time and he was gutted not to be playing. He had been a regular in the side, but lost his place shortly before the final. I was fit, but not match fit, and I knew I would have been struggling had I got on. Maybe it is just as well I stayed on the bench. Not long before, I also turned down the chance to join Wigan Athletic on loan. I went to watch a game and had a chat with manager Bryan Hamilton, but didn't fancy it. I thought: What's the point coming at this time of the season? Besides, Oldham were doing well and I decided to stay, which proved to be the right decision.

It was a bonus to be involved in the final as well as the two great runs in the Littlewoods Cup and FA Cup, even though I didn't play as much as I would have liked. It was great to be involved in a final at Wembley and it was amazing travelling and seeing the hordes of people from Oldham. There were even 50 or 60 from Bristol, my home city, who had come to shout for Latics.

My lasting memory is what a hot day it was for April. I heard it mentioned it was 100 degrees in the stadium. And I shall never forget Joe Royle had me warming up for an hour, even though I never got on to the pitch. While it was a great day for the club and for Oldham, it was disappointing we failed to win. From what I can remember, it was not a great game and too many of our players didn't perform on the day. It was as though some froze as they were up against a Nottingham Forest side containing Stuart Pearce and some other big names. We certainly didn't play to the level we did when beating the likes of Arsenal, Southampton, Everton and Aston Villa. That could also have been down to it being near the end of a 65-game marathon.

At the end of the season, there was an almighty sigh of relief that it was finally over because it was as though it was never ending. I can remember the disappointment of losing, though that didn't seem to matter to the fans who had a great day out. And what an amazing homecoming we received with an open-top bus parade and civic reception. It was as though the whole town was out to greet us.

Moulden's watching brief

Paul Moulden found himself in the unenviable position of joining Latics from Bournemouth for a club record £225,000 in March 1990 and being ineligible to play in both the Littlewoods Cup and FA Cup. Yet, as Moulden explained, he almost unwittingly found himself part of the team who played in the semi-final of the FA Cup against Manchester United.

The team were training for the FA Cup semi-final when, because of the things we

PAUL MOULDEN

Paul Moulden has been just itching to score his first goal for the Latics. Like all strikers, he knows that once the first one has gone in the others, somehow, seem easier to get.

He went through a similar experience in his Manchester City days. During his apprenticeship days at Maine Road Paul played for the England youth team and he got his chance in City's senior team for a Full Members' Cup tie against Sunderland in November 1985. Though he got a couple of outings in their First Division side during the course of that season it was in 1986/87 that he began to establish himself.

It was almost a year after his first appearance that Paul registered his first senior goal for City. Playing against Wimbledon in another Full Members' Cup tie, he contributed two goals to a 3-1 victory.

Four days later he grabbed two more in a 3-1 First Division victory over Aston Villa. He scored again in his next game against Charlton.

"It does something for the confidence when that first one goes in," said Paul at the time.

Paul scored eight times in 1986/87 but found himself back in the reserves for much of the following season.

It was in 1988/89 that he really made his mark with City. He scored steadily throughout their Second Division promotion winning campaign and registered his first hat-trick in a 4-2 win over Sheffield United in the Littlewoods Cup.

Paul, having ended the season top scorer with 17 goals, was looking forward to a return to the First Division.

So it came as a surprise when he learned that City were prepared to sell him. In one of their closing games of the season, Paul had netted twice against Bournemouth and his overall performance impressed their manager Harry Redknapp so much that he made a £300,000 bid for the player.

Paul, who had been impressed with Bournemouth's attitude and style they pulled back from 0-3 to draw 3-3 at Maine Road agreed to move south.

"When I visited Dean Court I was impressed by their professionalism and their ambition," said Paul.

He opened his account for the Cherries with a goal in a 1-1 draw with West Bromwich. In his next game he hit a hat-trick against Hull.

Again it was a case of, once the first one had gone in, everything else seemed to follow.

Playing alongside former England forward Luther Blissett, Paul contributed to one of the more impressive striking partnerships in the Second Division last season.

When the Latics were hit by that crippling series of injuries, manager Joe Royle moved in to sign him in March. He had scored 13 times for Bournemouth when he left.

Now he just wants to get off the mark with the Latics.

VITAL PROGRAMMING......Paul Moulden featured in Latics' match-day publication.

had been doing, I clocked I was in the squad for the next day's big match against Manchester United. I knew I had played for Bournemouth in the FA Cup that season, if only for 16 or 17 minutes as a sub after recovering from an ankle injury. I raised the matter with Joe Royle, who told me the secretary, Terry Cale, had checked and insisted I was all clear to play. But this was wrong. Obviously, I wasn't eligible and I didn't figure. If I had not said anything, I would have been on the team sheet. I'm sure some players might have stayed silent because it is not every day you get the chance to play in the semi-finals of the FA Cup. I often wonder what might have happened had I played in the game?

I jumped at the chance to join Latics as it meant a move to the North West, where I was raised. Bournemouth had spent heavily trying for promotion to the First Division and had been near the top most of the season. I think the money had dried up and there were also a lot of injuries. Harry Redknapp made it clear he needed new bodies and said one of us would leave before the transfer deadline. It turned out to be me. A number of clubs were interested and Oldham looked a good move with them doing so well.

When I arrived, the place was buzzing, as you would expect given their success in the Littlewoods Cup and FA Cup. But it turned out to be difficult and frustrating for me as I was ineligible in the cups and, for the league games, you could hardly expect Joe to leave out players who had done so well. Besides, Latics already had some very good forwards. There were no complaints from me. It did feel strange, however, and I was like an outsider gatecrashing the party. But I had nothing against anybody and they were a smashing set of lads who welcomed me. It goes without saying I would love to have been part of the cup runs, but it was not to be. It was still great to be at the club during the most exciting chapters in their history.

Dream move for Redders

Neil Redfearn joined Latics from Watford for £150,000 in January, 1990 in good time for the start of the FA Cup campaign, though he was ineligible for the Littlewoods Cup, thereby missing out on a Wembley appearance.

WATCHING BRIEF....new-signing Neil Redfearn was ineligible for the Littlewoods Cup campaign.

It was certainly an exciting time to be joining Latics, who were already through to the quarter-finals of the Littlewoods Cup. The season was gathering momentum and every other game was a big one with crowds of 17,000/18,000 packed into Boundary Park. What I will always remember was how vocal the fans were. They made more noise than 40,000 elsewhere. With being ineligible to play in the Littlewoods Cup, it was frustrating when those ties came around, as was missing out on the chance to play at Wembley. But at least I got to feature in the semi-final of the FA Cup and we were involved in two magnificent games against Manchester United which went to extra time. The matches had everything, great goals and great football, and it is a measure of how good they were that people are still talking about them 20 years later. It was big Manchester against little Manchester, but we more than matched them over the two ties. And, with a slice of luck, we could have won. Here I am thinking of Nick Henry's shot early in the replay which bounced down off the crossbar and which we felt was two feet over the line. If that goal had been given, it could well have got us to the final. But, over the two games, we played ever so well.

Alex Ferguson was under immense pressure at that time as he had not won anything since he was appointed three and a half years earlier. And it is amazing that United's dominance over the last two decades possibly hinged on that game as they went on to lift the cup. It was difficult for Joe Royle bringing me in mid-way through the season as I couldn't play in the Littlewoods Cup and, after a win, he would often stick with the same team. I would find it frustrating when those cup-ties came around and it was a case of having to be patient. When a side are successful, however, you are prepared to be more patient and I was glad to be involved at such an exciting time. In fairness to Joe, he played me as much as he could and featuring in the FA Cup semi-final and replay were the two biggest matches I ever played in.

I went on to become a permanent fixture the next season when I scored 18 goals in the Second Division title-winning campaign, including the injury-time penalty winner on the last day of the season against Sheffield Wednesday that won us the championship. When I look back on the 20 months I had with Latics, it was the most successful chapter in my career because of what I achieved in such a short space of time.

Scott's bitter-sweet season

Scott McGarvey has bitter-sweet memories of the 1989/90 season, having signed in the close season from Bristol City in a £22,000 transfer. He failed to establish a regular place and even spent a short loan spell at Wigan Athletic before moving on the next summer to Japanese club Mazda, who were managed by Manchester United legend Bill Foulkes.

While it was probably the greatest year Oldham have ever had, that certainly wasn't the case for me. Personally, it was one of the worst. I had only been at Oldham two months when I learned that my father Tommy was terminally ill and did not have long to live – something which knocked me for six. It was therefore a difficult time for me off the field because my life had been turned upside down.

In saying that, I loved the season I had at the club. I wished it had been longer, but sadly things did not work out as sometimes happens in football. There was an abundance of strikers when you looked at Andy Ritchie, Frank Bunn and Roger Palmer while defenders Paul Warhurst and Ian Marshall were equally at home up front. And, to be brutally honest, I was not playing well enough to be a regular in the team, though I made six starts and 12 substitute appearances that season. Joe Royle was a brilliant manager and the squad of players he had assembled would have graced the Premier League today. It was a great side and, had they been in the Championship at this moment in time, they would have been top of the table.

We had such a strong dressing room in which there were no weak characters and many of the lads weren't afraid to give their opinions. One of my most vivid memories of that season was the Littlewoods Cup quarter final against Southampton. I was a substitute at The Dell, where I went on after an hour, and I will never forget the drama of Andy Ritchie equalising in the fourth minute of injury-time to earn a replay. It was a brilliant game. That trip also provided an amusing little story as we came back from Southampton that night by private jet. I rang my mate 'Muzzer', who had a pub in Cheetham Hill and told him to save a pint for me as the pub would be closed. I knocked on the door and went in to find the customers watching the highlights of the game on ITV and the old guys standing at the bar could not figure out how I had got back from Southampton so quickly.

I got to start the replay at Boundary Park, where we finished the job beating the Saints, who were then a leading First Division club. And though things did not go well for me personally that season, it was still brilliant to be part of the team who reached the final of the Littlewoods Cup and semi-finals of the FA Cup as a Second Division side.

Wayne's watching brief

Wayne Heseltine suffered the heartbreak of breaking his leg not long after his £40,000 transfer from Manchester United, an injury which kept him on the sidelines for most of the big cup clashes.

When I signed from Manchester United in the October, there was no inkling as to how the season would pan out. We were still then only in the early stages of the Littlewoods Cup and the FA Cup had not begun for league clubs. I was excited to have made the move because I thought it would increase my chances of getting regular first-team football. I had only been with Latics for six weeks and was settling in nicely when I broke my leg, which was the end of my season and a massive disappointment when you consider what happened later. While I was pleased that the team were doing so well, the biggest downside was not being involved. It was very frustrating.

There were times when I was down in the dumps. The build-up to the final of the Littlewoods Cup was great and there was a good atmosphere and buzz about the club. And it was a good experience to be involved in the preparations for a final, though, obviously, something was missing due to the fact I was unable to play.

Apprentice fired by success

Chris Makin was an apprentice at Boundary Park, making his league debut in the final game of the season at Bradford City.

When I look at how Latics are struggling today, it is hard to believe what the team achieved 20 years ago. I may have only been an apprentice, but it was still great to be around the club at that time. I had been at Manchester United's centre of excellence before joining Latics and I would stand in the Chaddy End watching games. I had begun to see Joe Royle putting his stamp on the club, so the success was no surprise, though nobody expected anything on the scale of what happened in 1989/90. That season was amazing and I was at a lot of the big cup matches when we beat the likes of Arsenal and Aston Villa. And who will ever forget the 6-0 win against West Ham in the Littlewoods Cup semi-finals? I can still vividly picture the lengthy queues for tickets at Boundary Park when they were due to go on sale for some of the big cup games.

The young apprentices and professionals also went to the final at Wembley, which was another of those days I will never forget. We had a good youth team, including Paul Bernard and Paul Gerrard, who also went on to become first-team regulars. Nearly all visiting teams hated playing on the plastic pitch and it is true that many of them were beaten even before the match kicked off. We had numerous players who were at ease on the surface and who produced some unbelievable attacking football, which was a joy to watch. The 'pinch-me season' was only the start of five magical years in which we won promotion the following season and then had three years playing in the top flight. It was boom time at the club. Oldham became everyone's second team and what we achieved captured the imagination of the nation. What I will never forget about that time was the atmosphere at those big cup games, which was electric.

Kiwi adventure cut short

Chris Blundell was recalled from a loan spell in New Zealand due to a defensive injury crisis.

I was a second-year professional and had been on loan in New Zealand when I was called back to Boundary Park in October just as the Littlewoods Cup run was gathering pace. Though I only played one first-team game that season, it was still great to be involved on the sidelines. I loved being able to train alongside the likes of Roger Palmer, Andy Ritchie and Frank Bunn. Latics had some very good players at that time and many went on to play at a higher level. Sadly, the same didn't happen to me as I later joined Rochdale before drifting into non-league football with Northwich Victoria and Winsford United. But I still have great memories of that season and what made it extra special was being a member of the playing squad.

League campaign match by match

Saturday, August 19th, 1989
Blackburn Rovers 1 (Garner), Latics 0

First-day flop

It was hardly the most auspicious start for Latics, who kicked off the new campaign with a derby defeat. And the headline from the Oldham Evening Chronicle – 'Latics in first-day flop at Ewood' – summed up the match succinctly without the need to read too much of the report. The game was eminently forgettable as Latics, renowned for their attacking prowess, hardly troubled home keeper Terry Gennoe all afternoon.

The only promise came from Rick Holden with an encouraging debut following his £165,000 transfer from Watford two days earlier. Holden, who had hardly trained with his new team-mates, produced flashes of brilliance which suggested he would become a fans' favourite at Boundary Park. Latics failed to improve on their dismal record at Ewood as they went down to a fourth-minute goal from Simon Garner. Keeper Andy Rhodes raced out of the penalty area as Tony Finnigan burst through on goal. Sadly, he miscued his clearance to Garner, who drove home a shot from 25 yards. Holden came the closest to scoring for Latics with a chip which was kept out by a brilliant one-handed save from Gennoe.

LATICS: Rhodes, Irwin, Barlow, Henry, Barrett, A Holden, Adams (Palmer 55), Ritchie, Bunn (Marshall 65), Milligan, R Holden.

RICK HOLDEN....soon shone on Oldham's left.

Tuesday, August 22nd, 1989
Latics 1 (R Holden), Watford 1 (Dean Holdsworth)

Rick's major impact

Rick Holden marked his home debut with the goal which earned Latics their first point of the season. And it was a sweet moment for the 24-year-old winger, who had moved from Watford to Boundary Park only five days earlier. Latics produced a much-improved performance but it was still not good enough to defeat the Hornets. Holden broke the deadlock after 35 minutes when the Watford defence failed to clear a Denis Irwin cross and, in the ensuing mayhem, the winger swivelled before firing home a close-range shot.

Instead of building on the goal and using it as a platform for victory, Latics allowed Watford back into the game after a piece of charitable defending as last season's failings at the back resurfaced. Dean Holdsworth was left unmarked from a Glenn Roeder free-kick early in the second half as he was afforded time on the edge of the box to control the ball and pick his spot. Holden thought he had scored a 78th minute winner, only to see his effort ruled out for offside. Referee Alan Seville signalled a goal, but he was alerted to a flag from his linesman, who had spotted the infringement. Watford manager Steve Harrison conceded it was a brave decision by the match official.

LATICS: Rhodes, Irwin, Barrett, Palmer, Marshall, A Holden, Adams, Ritchie, Bunn, Milligan, R Holden. Subs (not used): Barlow, Henry.

Saturday, August 26th, 1989
Latics 2 (Palmer 2), Swindon Town 2 (McLoughlin, Shearer)

Roger to the rescue

It took a double strike from Roger Palmer to rescue a point for Latics, who found themselves 2-0 down early in the second half. Palmer inspired the comeback after a ponderous opening in which Swindon built a two-goal lead through goals from former Boundary Park Juniors' player Alan McLoughlin and Duncan Shearer. It was only after Shearer struck the second goal early in the second half that it jolted Latics to their senses as they again struggled to find the right shape or balance to their team. And it was a half-time substitution from manager Joe Royle which helped bring about the transformation. Nick Henry replaced Neil Adams – a move which enabled Palmer to switch from central midfield to the right flank, from where he caused so much trouble by ghosting into goalscoring positions.

Palmer lifted spirits after 66 minutes with a clinical piece of finishing which set up a rousing finish. Latics, galvanised by the goal, might even have snatched a victory which had looked improbable after an opening hour in which they toiled to find any fluency or pattern to their play. Following a succession of misses, they struck the equaliser eight minutes from time after Swindon player-manager Ossie Ardiles lost possession. Rick Holden whipped in a cross from the left, Frank Bunn challenged keeper Fraser Digby and, as the ball broke free, the predatory Palmer was on hand to volley home from close range.

LATICS: Rhodes, Irwin, Barrett, Palmer, Marshall (Barlow 58), A Holden, Adams (Henry 45), Ritchie, Bunn, Milligan, R Holden.

<<<◇>>>

Saturday, September 2nd, 1989
Newcastle United 2 (Quinn 2), Latics 1 (R Holden)

Mighty Quinn

Latics old-boy Mick Quinn inflicted further pain and misery on his former club in their defeat at St James' Park. Quinn continued his red-hot scoring streak following his £685,000 summer move from Portsmouth as he made it seven goals in only three matches – a run which quickly endeared him to the soccer-mad Geordies. That was little consolation to Royle, who had bought him from Stockport for £52,000 in 1984 and sold him for three times that amount two years later to Pompey. Quinn was the difference between the two teams and Latics considered themselves unlucky to leave the North East empty-handed after a performance which provided optimism for the remainder of the season.

They were without the injured Andy Holden and Ian Marshall, their usual centre-back combination, as left-back Earl Barrett and Paul Warhurst were paired together in the centre of defence for the first time. It looked as though Latics would safely negotiate the opening period until Quinn rifled home an unstoppable shot a minute before the break. They drew level shortly after the hour when Rick Holden struck with a spectacular overhead kick following a cross from left-back Andy Barlow. Just when it looked as though Latics were getting on top, referee Keith Hackett ruled that Warhurst had handled and Quinn scored from the penalty spot to seal victory.

LATICS: Rhodes, Irwin, Barlow, Henry, Barrett, Warhurst, Palmer, Ritchie, Bunn (Williams 65), Milligan, R Holden. Sub (not used): Donachie.

<<<<>>>

Saturday, September 9th, 1989
Latics 3 (Palmer, R Holden, Ritchie), Plymouth Argyle 2 (McCarthy, Thomas)

Off the mark

Lowly Latics recorded their first league victory, at the fifth attempt, but it was not without some anxious moments. The win should have been resounding as they hit the woodwork four times and threatened an avalanche of goals. But defensive frailties concerned Joe Royle, who admitted the game had knocked six months off his life. "We must be the most creative team in the country…the only trouble is that it is at both ends," he declared, admitting Plymouth had two glorious late chances to level.

Andy Ritchie, Rick Holden and Mike Milligan hit the post or bar before Roger Palmer fired Latics ahead. They were stunned early in the second half, though, when Sean McCarthy, who would some years later join them from Bradford City, equalised in a rare Plymouth sortie. Holden quickly restored Latics' lead with his third goal in five games since his £165,000 transfer from Watford. Ritchie was denied by the frame of the goal for a second time before finally finding the net as he intercepted a poor throw by keeper Rhys Wilmot. The two-goal cushion was halved almost immediately when Andy Thomas scored from a well-rehearsed free-kick to set up a nervous last 19 minutes in which Tommy Tynan and Mark Stuart had good chances.

LATICS: Rhodes, Irwin, Barlow, Henry, Barrett, Warhurst, Palmer, Ritchie, Bunn, Milligan, R Holden. Subs (not used): Williams, Donachie.

112

Saturday, September 16th, 1989
Stoke City 1 (Bamber), Latics 2 (Palmer, Ritchie)

First away-day win

It was like waiting for a bus as, after a lengthy wait for their first league win, Latics made it back-to-back victories. Their first away win of the season came against a Stoke side who had spent £900,000 rebuilding their squad in the summer. Manager Royle was particularly impressed by a vastly improved defensive display as the Potters were restricted to a handful of chances. Latics lived dangerously early on, but weathered the storm to take a 17th minute lead when Palmer headed a Rick Holden corner past keeper Peter Fox to change the course of the game.

They doubled their advantage shortly before the break when left-back Derek Statham slipped as Stoke pushed out, looking for offside. This enabled Latics to spring the trap, with Ritchie cracking a rising drive past Fox. In those days, Latics were never more dangerous to themselves than while seemingly in control and they provided Stoke with a toe-hold back into the match midway through the second half when Dave Bamber halved the deficit. Stoke made a determined pursuit of an equaliser yet it was Latics who looked likeliest to score again in a number of dangerous counter-attacks.

LATICS: Rhodes, Irwin, Barlow, Henry, Marshall, Barrett, Palmer, Ritchie, Bunn, Milligan, R Holden. Subs (not used): Warhurst, Williams.

Saturday, September 23rd, 1989
Latics 2 (Ritchie 2), West Bromwich Albion 1 (West)

Climbing high

Following their erratic start to the season, Latics' hard-earned victory over West Brom lifted them to seventh place in the table. Such was the tightness of the division that they suddenly found themselves only four points behind leaders Sheffield United, their next opponents. Latics failed to deliver their best form in what turned out to be a rugged and scrappy affair and it took them almost an hour to find a breakthrough –

and even then it was from a penalty by the ever-reliable Andy Ritchie after a linesman flagged to indicate that defender Stacey North had handled.

The Baggies drew level only nine minutes later when striker Colin West's header squirmed through the hands of keeper Andy Rhodes. Latics had to prise open a tight visiting defence again and managed to do so when North and keeper Andy Marriott got in a tangle following a Denis Irwin cross and Ritchie struck again. Paul Warhurst's late dismissal for striking West off the ball meant it was a nervy final eight minutes for the 10 men remaining and West almost took full advantage by conjuring up an equaliser.

LATICS: Rhodes, Irwin, Barlow, Henry, Barrett, Warhurst, Palmer, Ritchie, Bunn, Milligan, R Holden. Subs (not used): Williams, Donachie.

<<<<>>>>

Tuesday, September 26th, 1989
Sheffield United 2 (Deane, Agana), Latics 1 (Bunn)

Blades cut it

Latics appeared to be within touching distance of a point at leaders Sheffield United when a dour match burst into life with an explosive finish. The game appeared to be meandering towards a tame goalless draw when Dave Bassett's route-one side snatched victory with two quick-fire goals which inflicted the first defeat on Latics for five matches. Only 13 minutes remained when the Blades cut a path to the Latics goal as Tony Agana headed on a John Gannon free-kick and Brian Deane, ghosting in at the far post, guided a shot past keeper Andy Rhodes.

They sealed victory four minutes later when Deane repaid the compliment by setting up Agana, who burst past Earl Barrett to fire home and preserve their three-point lead at the top of the table. Frank Bunn's goal two minutes from time, a header from a Rick Holden cross, proved nothing more than a consolation, though it was the striker's first goal of the campaign. Sadly, the concentrated action of the final 13 minutes was hardly enough to make up for the dismal nature of the previous 77.

LATICS: Rhodes, Irwin, Barlow, Henry, Warhurst, Barrett, Palmer, Ritchie, Bunn, Milligan, R Holden. Subs (not used): Williams, Donachie.

Saturday, September 30th, 1989
Latics 1 (Morgan og), Leicester City 0

Own goal decider

Latics laboured as they beat bottom-of-the-table Leicester thanks to a goal from one of the Foxes players. It was one of those rare days when Latics lost their bearings in front of goal. And it was left to Leicester defender Simon Morgan to show how it should be done. Frank Bunn drove the ball across the face of goal in the 54th minute, only to see it bounce off the unfortunate Morgan past stranded keeper Martin Hodge.

The win – their fifth in six league and cup matches – was the perfect pick-me-up after the midweek defeat at Bramall Lane. And recalled keeper Jon Hallworth, playing his first match of the season after recovering from injury, marked his return with a clean sheet, the first Latics had achieved in 10 competitive matches. Hallworth had rarely had an easier day's work as Leicester found Latics' defence in uncompromising mood, with Earl Barrett and Ian Marshall, who was also returning after injury, hardly putting a foot wrong. Paul Kitson went close, however, to snatching a late equaliser for the Foxes and, had he found the net, Latics would have been left cursing their string of missed scoring opportunities on a day when the importance of keeping a clean sheet was driven home.

LATICS: Hallworth, Irwin, Barlow, Henry, Marshall, Barrett, Palmer, Ritchie, Bunn, Milligan, R Holden. Subs (not used): Adams, Warhurst.

<<<<>>>>

Saturday, October 7th, 1989
Latics 2 (Bunn, Milligan), Barnsley 0

Seventh heaven

What made Latics' seventh victory in eight games – their best run since Joe Royle was appointed manager in 1982 – even more satisfying was that it was achieved with a severely depleted defence. Jon Hallworth, Ian Marshall and Andy Holden were all on the sidelines through injury while Paul Warhurst was suspended. And keeper Andy Rhodes overcome the inconvenience of a damaged finger to take his place. It was a

115

case of Royle juggling his back-line as best he could, with his 38-year-old player-coach Willie Donachie, who normally played at left-back, turning out as an emergency right-back while the dependable Denis Irwin switched from the flank and filled the unusual role of makeshift central defender. Indeed, it was probably the smallest back four in the club's history, with Earl Barrett the tallest member of it at a less than towering 5ft 10in.

EARL BARRETT
.....a giant at 5ft 10in.

By hook or by crook, the changes worked as Latics shut out the highly-rated strike-force of David Currie and Steve Cooper and the Tykes seldom threatened. Latics made a dream start, taking a fourth-minute lead when keeper Ian Wardle failed to hold a free-kick from Irwin, leaving Bunn to tuck away the loose ball. It was soon 2-0 when Wardle failed to hold another screaming shot from Irwin and this time Mike Milligan pounced to knock in his first goal of the season to put Latics in a commanding position with only seven minutes played. There was no way back for Barnsley as Latics recorded a fifth straight home win in league and cup.

LATICS: Rhodes, Donachie, Irwin, Barrett, Barlow, Palmer, Milligan, Henry, R Holden, Bunn, Ritchie. Subs (not used): Williams, Mooney.

<<<◇>>>

Saturday, October 14th, 1989
Bournemouth 2 (Moulden, Peacock), Latics 0

Away-day worries

Paul Moulden, who five months later would become a Latics player, was the architect of their undoing at Dean Court. The striker took only three minutes to find a hole in a still-below-strength defence as he scored his eighth goal of the season – a near-post diving header from a Shaun Brooks free-kick. It was a massively disappointing display as Latics slipped to only their second defeat in nine matches, but their form away from Boundary Park remained a worry. They had lost four of their six games on the road in league and cup, a considerable handicap in their bid to mount a bid for promotion.

And, but for an inspired display by keeper Andy Rhodes, it would have been an even heavier defeat as the Cherries picked holes in the Latics back-line; understandable given the continued problems with personnel in that area. What was even more worrying was Latics' failure to trouble Bournemouth, the team with the leakiest defence in the Second Division, as they hardly tested keeper Gerry Peyton all afternoon. Gavin Peacock sealed victory for the Cherries midway through the second half as he ran at the Latics defence before rifling home a low shot from the edge of the box.

LATICS: Rhodes, Irwin, Barlow (Adams 75), Henry, Donachie, Barrett, Palmer, Ritchie, Bunn, Milligan, R Holden. Sub (not used): Williams.

<<<◇>>>

Tuesday, October 17th, 1989
Hull City 0, Latics 0

Toothless Tigers

Latics' strikers were said to have gone into early hibernation as they failed to find the net for the second successive game, this time against a struggling Hull side who ought to have been ripe for the taking. As the final whistle sounded, the Tigers had extended their win-less sequence in the league to an incredible 23 games, the worst run in their history. Latics were described as playing like a team lacking ambition and one who didn't particularly want to win while Hull had no confidence. Put those two factors together and the Oldham Evening Chronicle's Bob Young referred to what he witnessed as "a right load of rubbish."

It was mentioned that Latics unquestionably had talent and flair in their side, but too many players seemed reluctant to show it. Indeed, they would have finished empty-handed but for a brilliant last minute point-blank save from Andy Rhodes to keep out Peter Swan's header. Latics' best opening of the game also came in the latter stages, when Rick Holden chipped keeper Iain Hesford, but his effort hit the top of the bar.

LATICS: Rhodes, Irwin, Barlow, Henry, Donachie, Barrett, Palmer, Ritchie, Bunn, Milligan, R Holden. Subs (not used): Williams, Adams.

Saturday, October 21st, 1989
Latics 2 (Ritchie 2), Middlesbrough 0

Ritchie at the double

Joe Royle was far from impressed, though Andy Ritchie's double brought about a return to winning ways against struggling Middlesbrough. "We were functional rather than sparkling, but, in a division as tight as ours, you have to be able to pick up points when you are not at your best," said the Latics manager. "We've played worse than that and won, but we have also played much better and lost. At least we are up there among the leading group without having had the benefit of a settled side and knowing we still have good players on the way back to challenge for places."

Despite the indifferent form, it was Latics' fifth straight home league win and hoisted them to seventh, only seven points behind leaders Sheffield United. Their defending was good, with Andy Rhodes keeping a third clean sheet in four matches since his recall for the injured Jon Hallworth. He had little to do before saving superbly with 10 minutes left to deny striker Bernie Slaven and preserve his side's one-goal lead. Latics took the lead mid-way through the opening half when Boro keeper Kevin Poole failed to catch a cross from Rick Holden and left Ritchie with the simple task of chesting home. They were worth more than their slender advantage at the break, having carved out a succession of clear-cut chances. Amazingly, it was not until the 85th minute that Ritchie secured victory with a powerful header, his eighth goal of the season, following a pinpoint cross from Rick Holden.

LATICS: Rhodes, Irwin, Barlow, Henry, Warhurst, Barrett, Palmer, Ritchie, Bunn, Milligan, R Holden. Subs (not used): Adams, Donachie.

Saturday, October 28th, 1989
Wolverhampton Wanderers 1 (Thompson pen), Latics 1 (Milligan)

Milligan magic

Latics' performance at Molineux was described as more potent and purposeful than in previous matches on their travels. After a rocky start, in which keeper Andy

Rhodes made two splendid saves, Latics more than held their own against mid-table Wolves. But they had the misfortune of falling behind seven minutes into the second half after a handball by Paul Warhurst. Rhodes saved Thompson's spot-kick, only for referee Ray Lewis to order a retake for encroachment and for the same player to hold his nerve and this time score.

Latics were unlucky not to equalise when Rick Holden's shot was deflected off a defender and against the bar. It was no surprise when they deservedly drew level in the 69th minute, Nick Henry pulling back a low cross for Mike Milligan to fire home from the edge of the box. And Royle's men might have snatched victory late on against a club who had won promotion in each of the previous two seasons, with Andy Ritchie, put through on goal by Denis Irwin, shooting wide.

LATICS: Rhodes, Irwin, Barlow, Henry, Barrett, Warhurst, Palmer, Ritchie, Bunn, Milligan, R Holden. Subs (not used): Williams, Donachie.

<<<<◇>>>

Tuesday, October 31st, 1989
Latics 2 (Barlow, Ritchie), Bradford City 2 (Quinn 2)

Record under threat

Latics' nine-month unbeaten home record came under threat as Andy Ritchie rescued a draw with a late penalty in a game in which they twice came from behind to snatch a point. Bradford City went as close as any team to inflicting a first home loss in 20 matches on Latics as they proved again they were at ease on the artificial surface. They had lost there only once in four visits. Latics were far from their best and could have had no complaints had Bradford registered the first win by a visiting side at Boundary Park since Manchester City's triumph early in the year, the absence of four of their tallest players proving a handicap against one of the strongest sides in the Second Division.

Jimmy Quinn fired Bradford ahead after eight minutes with a spectacular free-kick from 30 yards and it might well have been worse had keeper Andy Rhodes not pulled off a super save to deny the same player. Manager Joe Royle's gamble in pushing left-back Andy Barlow into midfield and playing most of the second period with three defenders paid dividends. It was Barlow who put Latics back on level terms in the 55th minute, ghosting in at the far post to squeeze home a cross from Roger Palmer and score his first goal for 20 months. The joy was short-lived as Bradford regained the lead within three minutes when Quinn struck for a second time, firing home a cross from Brian Mitchell. It looked as though it was not going to be Latics' day when Ritchie was denied by the upright, but their patience was eventually rewarded when they won a 72nd minute penalty. Referee Mike Reed ruled Ritchie had been shoved and the striker picked himself up to score his 10th goal of the season. Latics had chances to secure a ninth straight home victory as Palmer was denied what appeared a blatant penalty while Ritchie was frustrated by a superb one-handed save from Paul Tomlinson.

LATICS: Rhodes, Irwin, Barlow, Henry, Barrett, Warhurst, Adams, Ritchie, Palmer, Milligan, R Holden. Subs (not used): Williams, Donachie.

<<<<>>>>

Saturday, November 4th, 1989
Latics 2 (Warhurst, Ritchie), Sunderland 1 (Owers)

Quality Street

Quality Street was how one newspaper headline described Latics' victory against third-placed Sunderland – a win which put them firmly in the chase for a play-off place. It was an important success against one of the favourites for promotion and enhanced their own credentials in a match which was referred to as a cracking contest. Latics' eighth home win from nine games was secured by spectacular strikes from the ever-reliable Ritchie and a first goal in professional football from 20-year-old defender Paul Warhurst.

Ritchie gave Latics the perfect start with a stunning overhead kick from a Denis Irwin delivery. Warhurst, making only his 10th first-team appearance, doubled their advantage early in the second half in equally spectacular style. Rick Holden's cross was cleared to Warhurst, who spotted keeper Tim Carter off his line and beat him from outside the box with the most delicate of chips. Latics created a hatful of chances, only to be denied time and time again by either Carter's heroics or often desperate defending while Sunderland also had their moments, but found keeper Andy Rhodes in fine form. The visitors did pull a goal back two minutes from time through

Gary Owers with a delightful lob over Rhodes from 25 yards, but it proved too little, too late as Sunderland suffered their first defeat in five matches. After Latics' draws at Wolves and at home to Bradford in their two previous league matches, this was considered a vital victory, one that was needed to keep them on the shirt tails of the top teams.

LATICS: Rhodes, Irwin, Barlow, Henry, Barrett, Warhurst, Palmer, Ritchie, Marshall, Milligan, R Holden. Subs (not used): Adams, Williams.

<<<<>>>>

Saturday, November 11th, 1989
Oxford United 0, Latics 1 (Ritchie)

Lord Ritchie

'Ritchie is Lord of the Manor' was the perfect headline as Latics recorded only their second away win on their 1989/90 league travels. Ritchie came up with the all-important goal at the Manor Ground, his 12th of the season, as Latics matched the previous season's disappointing total of away league victories. It was a performance which oozed class and the only surprise was that the triumph did not come by a wider margin as the impressive run of results was stretched to only one defeat in 11 competitive matches. There was plenty to cheer for Latics at both ends of the pitch as they clearly showed they had the firepower to challenge for promotion while proving they had also tightened things at the back.

This was the club's sixth clean sheet in 11 matches, a remarkable achievement bearing in mind all of their injury troubles at the back. The decisive goal came after 25 minutes following a sweeping move which went almost the full length of the sloping Manor Ground and finished when Ritchie found the net with a rasping shot from 12 yards. There was still an anxious moment to be negotiated because a linesman had his flag raised for offside against Rick Holden. But referee David Elleray thankfully ruled that the winger was not interfering with play and so allowed the goal to stand.

LATICS: Rhodes, Irwin, Barlow, Henry, Barrett, Warhurst (Marshall 46), Palmer, Ritchie, Bunn, Milligan, R Holden. Sub (not used): Williams.

'PINCH ME NOT'

Saturday, November 18th, 1989
Latics 1 (Milligan), Brighton & Hove Albion 1 (Codner)

Misses costly

Latics were left to reflect on the two costly points which slipped through their grasp as they were held at home by Brighton. It was a match they ought to have had wrapped up in a one-sided opening half in which all they had to show for their effort and endeavour was a solitary goal from Mike Milligan. They should have been at least three to the good as Brighton had the woodwork and keeper John Keeley to thanks for their slender deficit. Denis Irwin and Andy Ritchie were both denied by the frame of the goal, Roger Palmer had an effort cleared off the goal-line while Keeley pulled off smart saves to thwart Palmer and Ritchie.

Milligan's neatly-taken 39th minute goal followed a quickly-taken free kick by keeper Andy Rhodes, which released Ritchie on the right for the striker to set up the midfield man. Brighton equalised on the hour when Latics failed to clear a corner and Robert Codner fired home from the edge of the area, albeit with the aid of a deflection past Rhodes. Manager Joe Royle threw on defender Ian Marshall as a makeshift striker and he nearly conjured a match-winning goal 11 minutes from time. Keeley made a save which was compared to the one Gordon Banks made to deny Pele in the 1970 World Cup as he got down to Marshall's downward header and miraculously deflect the ball against the upright.

LATICS: Rhodes, Irwin, Barlow, Henry, Barrett, Warhurst, Palmer (Marshall 74), Ritchie, Bunn, Milligan, R Holden. Sub (not used): Williams.

Saturday, November 25th, 1989
Ipswich Town 1 (Kiwomya), Latics 1 (Yallop og)

Royle regret

Manager Royle was disappointed with this result, even though the in-form Suffolk side had six wins from their previous seven matches. It was a useful away point which stretched Latics' unbeaten run to 10 matches in league and cup and maintained their top-six spot. But Latics were a shadow of the side who beat champions Arsenal three days earlier in the Littlewoods Cup – understandable given the seismic scale of that achievement. The major problem on the side's travels was still a lack of goals, and even their one at Portman Road came courtesy of Ipswich's Frank Yallop. But, after the previous season's habit of leaking goals for fun, Latics could now boast the joint meanest defence in the Second Division as a measure of how their defensive play had improved.

After surviving a shaky start, Latics conceded an 18th minute penalty, but were furious as they claimed Louie Donowa dived for the spot-kick. Justice appeared to have been meted out, however, when keeper Andy Rhodes made a superb save low to his right to deny John Wark. Latics eventually woke from their slumbers and created a string of clear-cut chances, only to be let down by the lack of a cutting edge. They eventually made a 68th minute breakthrough when Rick Holden's in-swinging corner flew into the net off defender Yallop. Ipswich claimed the ball had not crossed the line, but a linesman signalled a goal. Latics were only ahead for five minutes as Ipswich quickly conjured an equaliser, Chris Kiwomya beating the offside trap and poking a shot past Rhodes.

LATICS: Rhodes, Irwin, Barlow, Henry, Warhurst, Barrett, Palmer, Ritchie, Marshall, Milligan, R Holden. Subs (not used): Adams, Williams.

<<<<>>>>

Friday, December 1st, 1989
Latics 2 (Holden, Ritchie), Blackburn Rovers 0

Please Joe, don't go

This was a highly emotional night at Boundary Park, where supporters made impassioned pleas for Joe Royle to stay. The Latics manager had emerged as a front-runner to succeed the sacked Mel Machin at Manchester City and fans paid for messages like 'Please Joe, Don't Go' to be flashed on the electronic scoreboard while others unfurled banners carrying similar messages. The Latics players weren't caught up in the frenzy, even though the mood was somewhat subdued. They remained focused on inflicting only a second away league defeat on Blackburn and achieved their aim in what was described as a functional rather than sparkling display.

'PINCH ME NOT'

Latics swept aside the challenge of their promotion rivals despite being without the injured Mike Milligan and Frank Bunn. The game wasn't much of a spectacle as Blackburn were content to defend for a draw while Latics failed to turn their superiority into goals. Ian Marshall, again used as a striker in the absence of Bunn, made a nuisance of himself and Nick Henry struck the bar. But Latics had to be patient before finally being rewarded on the hour when Rick Holden ended a 16-match spell without a goal as he popped up at the near post to turn in a cross from Andy Ritchie, who sealed victory himself nine minutes later. Neil Adams made a break down the right wing and Nick Henry laid back the ball for Ritchie to hammer home a fierce shot for his 15th goal of the season as Latics extended their unbeaten home run to a formidable 24 matches.

LATICS: Rhodes, Irwin, Barlow, Henry, Barrett, Warhurst, Adams, Ritchie, Marshall, Palmer, R Holden. Subs (not used): Williams, McGarvey.

<<<<>>>>

Saturday, December 9th, 1989
Watford 3 (Wilkinson, Hodges, Penrice), Latics 0

Hornets sting

Latics played some of their best football of the campaign, yet suffered their heaviest defeat of the season in a peculiar game. The Hornets displayed a sting in front of goal that Latics lacked, the visitors playing their opponents off the park for lengthy periods, only to be stung by first-half goals from Paul Wilkinson, Glyn Hodges and Gary Penrice. Manager Joe Royle said: "We will play worse than that this season and win. We dominated the game and they seldom troubled us. Take away the scoreline and it was totally one-sided. They put away their chances and then defended well in the second half when we put them under a tremendous amount of pressure."

Latics goalkeeper Andy Rhodes was almost a spectator throughout other than picking the ball out of the net while opposite number Tony Coton confirmed his standing as one of the country's top keepers by making a string of super saves. Though Latics found themselves struggling at the interval, they had more than matched Watford as Frank Bunn struck the upright and Coton denied both the same forward and Mike Milligan. Coton continued to be the star of the show in the second period by frustrating Milligan, Ian Marshall and Ritchie as Latics discovered it simply wasn't their day.

LATICS: Rhodes, Irwin, Barlow (Palmer 46), Henry, Barrett, Warhurst, Marshall, Ritchie, Bunn, Milligan, Holden. Sub (not used): Adams.

<<<<>>>

Saturday, December 16th, 1989
West Ham 0, Latics 2 (Milligan, Foster og)

Hammer blow

Latics claimed their third away league victory – and their most notable scalp to date – as they climbed to fourth place and reinforced their growing bid for promotion. With Leeds and Sheffield United threatening to break clear, it was vital for Latics to keep in touch with the top two, yet, curiously, their display was nowhere near as fluent as the one at Vicarage Road a week earlier. It was a point acknowledged by Royle, who said: "We did well and were always comfortable, but we played better at Watford and lost. We were better here in front of goal and also defended better, with Earl Barrett outstanding while Andy Rhodes made some good saves when needed." The manager had expressed concern earlier in the week about a defence who had leaked five goals in the two previous away games. He was also worried about his side's strike-rate on their travels, with only seven league goals netted before this victory. Latics responded by keeping a splendid clean sheet while also twice piercing the Hammers' defence.

It was a marvellous victory which might have been even more emphatic as Andy Ritchie and Denis Irwin failed to take clear-cut opportunities in the latter stages. Mike Milligan fired Latics ahead in only the fifth minute after West Ham defender Colin Foster failed to clear a clever cross from winger Rick Holden. And the side doubled their advantage after 16 minutes when Irwin's low cross skidded across the sodden goalmouth and deflected in off the unlucky Foster. Whenever the hosts threatened, they were thwarted by Rhodes, who was unbeatable, just as Watford's Tony Coton had been against Latics the previous week. It was a measure of the comprehensive nature of the visitors' victory, however, that disappointed home supporters were

125

streaming away from Upton Park with all of 15 minutes left, voicing their disapproval at their team's performance and defeat. If only they had known what pain still lay in store for them!

LATICS: Rhodes, Irwin, Barlow, Henry, Barrett, Warhurst (Palmer 35), Marshall, Ritchie, Bunn, Milligan, R Holden. Sub (not used): Adams.

<<<<>>>>

Tuesday, December 26th, 1989
Latics 2 (Adams, Barrett), Port Vale 1 (Parkin)

Christmas cracker

This was a festive fillip as Latics' narrow victory cemented their hold on fourth place. Earl Barrett also received a perfect present as he marked his 100th Football League appearance with his first goal. There was more cheer, with the match attracting the biggest home league attendance of the season, 11,274. It was another of those days when Latics ought to have won by a wider margin and Valiants manager John Rudge recognised the fact when he admitted his side had been given a first-half run-about and were fortunate only to be 1-0 down at the break. Latics had enough chances to be home and dry by the half-way point, but the only reward for their efforts up to then was a 29th minute goal from Neil Adams – a header from a Nick Henry cross. It was the winger's first league goal since his £100,000 summer signing from Everton.

Vale threatened more in the second half, but Latics doubled their advantage on the hour through Barrett, who stayed up-field following a corner to head home a cross from Rick Holden. Any hopes they had of coasting through the remainder of the match disappeared a couple of minutes later, though, when their defence dozed off and allowed defender Tim Parkin to halve the deficit with a glancing header that brought him his first goal for the club. Latics retained their composure and late on had a couple of clear-cut chances which, had they been taken, would have made it a comfortable victory.

LATICS: Rhodes, Irwin, Barlow, Henry, Barrett, Marshall, Adams, Ritchie, Bunn, Milligan, R Holden. Subs (not used): Palmer, Heseltine.

Saturday, December 30th, 1989
Latics 3 (Milligan 2, Palmer), Portsmouth 3 (Whittingham 3)

Great Guy

Former Army striker Guy Whittingham scored a hat-trick for Portsmouth, but Latics refused to be shot down. They displayed courage and a never-say-die attitude to scrap for a point and extend their unbeaten home run to 26 matches. In a game that was almost a step too far, they found themselves 2-0 down after only 10 minutes and 3-2 behind before being rescued by a late goal from Mike Milligan, Pompey having arrived on a high of their own after losing only once in eight matches – a run which had lifted them out of the relegation places after a disastrous start. Their brimming confidence showedwhen Whittingham fired home in each of their first two attacks.

Yet Latics found themselves back on level terms shortly after the half-hour mark following a spectacular long-range drive from Milligan and a typical poachers' effort from Roger Palmer, who had replaced the injured Ritchie early on. Whittingham completed a first half hat-trick and Latics had to wait until the 86th minute before Milligan went to the rescue with a close-range volley for the equaliser. It was no more than Latics deserved after peppering the Pompey goal in the second half. Keeper Alan Knight twice denied Neil Adams and also thwarted Milligan and Rick Holden with super saves while Palmer hit the upright with a header.

LATICS: Rhodes, Irwin, Barlow, Henry, Barrett, Marshall, Adams, Ritchie (Palmer 23), Bunn, Milligan, R Holden. Sub (not used): Heseltine.

Monday, January 1st, 1990
Leeds United 1 (Hendrie), Latics 1 (Palmer)

Late leveller

Latics were denied a second win of the season at Elland Road by a late equaliser from John Hendrie. It looked as though Latics would inflict a first home league defeat of the season on Leeds following their success three months earlier in the Littlewoods Cup. Jon Hallworth returned in goal after a three-month absence through injury –

ironically, his last appearance had been at the ground in the cup success. And thanks in no small way to his efforts, Latics extended their unbeaten record at Elland Road to five matches. Having weathered an early onslaught, they began to create chances and it was no surprise when they took the lead after 35minutes when Roger Palmer was left unmarked to head home a left-wing cross from Andy Barlow. It silenced the vast majority of fans in a 30,217 crowd as Latics again held a magical spell over their arch rivals.

They were content to defend in the second half and strike with their swift counter-attacks. They frustrated Leeds, who had almost given up hope when they came up with an unlikely leveller. Dylan Kerr swung over a hopeful cross from the left and a miscued clearance from Andy Barlow let in Hendrie to fire home the equaliser. While a point was not to be sniffed at, there was an overwhelming sense of disappointment that Latics failed to leave with all the spoils. Leeds appeared certainties for promotion, even at this mid-way stage of the season, and on the evidence of this New Year's Day clash, Latics ought not to be far away from them.

LATICS: Hallworth, Irwin, Barlow, Henry, Marshall, Barrett, Adams, Palmer, Bunn, Milligan, R Holden. Subs (not used): McGarvey, Heseltine.

Saturday, January 13th, 1990
Swindon Town 3 (White 2, McLoughlin), Latics 2 (McGarvey, Adams)

Out of tune

The Robins were positively chirping as they leapfrogged injury-hit Latics into third place as the Second Division promotion race hotted up. Latics were again without the injured Frank Bunn, Andy Ritchie, Paul Warhurst and Andy Barlow as they handed debuts to Wayne Heseltine and Neil Redfearn, the latter of whom had only completed a £150,000 transfer from Watford two days earlier. They had plenty of possession but obviously lacked a cutting edge in the absence of their normal front two and found themselves 2-0 down early in the second half. Manager Joe Royle went for broke by sending on striker Scott McGarvey for left-back Heseltine and once again opting for three at the back. And fortune so nearly favoured the brave as

Latics' adventurous approach was rewarded when they netted two second-half goals to give Swindon the fright of their lives.

Latics survived some anxious moments, including Ian Marshall making a goal-line clearance, before Swindon went ahead after 35 minutes. The offside trap was breached and midfield-man Alan McLoughlin, a former Boundary Park Juniors player, burst through on goal to score his 13th goal of the season. Latics conceded a second early in the second half when Steve Foley flicked on a corner and Steve White found the net with a header from point-blank range. If Swindon thought they were home and dry, they were sadly mistaken as Latics produced a rousing final half hour.

McGarvey certainly made a dramatic impact on his league debut as, in 39 minutes on the pitch, he scored one goal, set up another and smashed a shot against the crossbar.

He had only been on the field for 12 minutes when he halved the deficit with a diving header from a Rick Holden cross. McGarvey then thundered a free kick from 25 yards against the woodwork as Latics continued to surge forward at every opportunity. Swindon survived and went on to re-establish a two-goal advantage through a far-post header from White and it was easy to see why they were the leading scorers in the Second Division. But they had to survive an anxious final three minutes after Neil Adams reduced the deficit to 3-2 as Holden's cross was flicked on by McGarvey for the winger to volley home from six yards.

LATICS: Hallworth, Irwin, Heseltine (McGarvey 51), Henry, Marshall, Barrett, Adams, Palmer, Redfearn, Milligan, R Holden. Sub (not used): Williams.

Saturday, January 20th, 1990
Latics 1 (Ritchie), Newcastle United 1 (McGhee)

Shutting up shop

Joe Royle complained that Latics had become victims of their own success after being held at home by another of the fancied clubs. The manager pointed to the fact that Newcastle, along with so many other visiting teams, employed a five-man defence at Boundary Park. He added that it wasn't usually a worry, but had become more problematic due to Latics' injury troubles. It was the sixth time they had been held in 14 home league matches, though they extended their unbeaten record in all competitions at Boundary Park to 27 games over a 12-month period. Royle also reaffirmed his belief that his fourth-placed side could still claim an automatic promotion place, though they were eight points adrift of second-placed Sheffield United and had surrendered 12 points in those six drawn matches.

Latics were reinforced by the return of Andy Ritchie, Paul Warhurst and Andy Barlow, but still found the going tough and clearly lacked the physical presence of the still-sidelined Frank Bunn and Ian Marshall. Newcastle's John Burridge made a superb save after only two minutes to deny Neil Redfearn a goal on his home debut but, incredibly, neither goalkeeper made a save in the remaining 88 minutes of a dour contest. Latics broke the deadlock midway through the second period when Ritchie marked his return with his 16th goal of the season as he headed home a cross from Denis Irwin. The lead lasted only eight minutes before the defence was split by a through ball from Roy Aitken. John Gallagher burst clear on the right and his low cross was tapped in by Mark McGhee at the far post for his 11th of the campaign.

LATICS: Hallworth, Irwin (Adams 72), Barlow, Henry, Barrett, Warhurst, Redfearn, Ritchie, Palmer, Milligan, R Holden. Sub (not used): McGarvey.

Saturday, February 3rd, 1990
West Bromwich Albion 2 (Robson, West), Latics 2 (Ritchie, Palmer)

Muddy marvels

Latics proved they can play on any surface as they found The Hawthorns far removed from the plastic paradise at Boundary Park. Having twice fallen behind, the players ploughed over a surface which was described as a paddy field to pick up another point in their pursuit of promotion. Latics remained fourth and, sadly, the increasing number of draws meant they were failing to make any inroads into the lead held by the top teams, with second-placed Sheffield United remaining eight points clear. It took Latics a little time to adjust to the unfamiliar conditions and they fell behind in the second minute through a goal from Gary Robson. Once Latics settled, though, they produced the more purposeful football and it was no surprise when they equalised midway through the opening half. Rick Holden, bursting through on goal on to a Denis Irwin pass, was brought down by keeper Stuart Naylor for Andy Ritchie to score from the spot. It was his sixth goal in five matches and 21st of the season.

Latics began to get on top, but found some of the defending uncompromising as the Baggies fought to stay clear of the relegation places. Sensing West Brom were there for the taking, manager Joe Royle sent on Roger Palmer for Scott McGarvey midway through the second period. Before Palmer had touched the ball, however, the home side snatched the lead through a Colin West header. But their advantage lasted only three minutes as Latics again displayed resilience and determination not to be beaten. Neil Adams hit a post and Stacey North cleared off the line to deny Palmer, who eventually made it 2-2 with a header after Ritchie's shot ballooned into the air following a deflection off Palmer. Late on, both side could have conjured a match-winner. Robson forced Jon Hallworth to make a fine save while Ian Marshall and Nick Henry both went close for Latics.

LATICS: Hallworth, Irwin, Barlow, Henry, Marshall, Barrett, Adams, Ritchie, McGarvey (Palmer 66), Milligan, R Holden. Sub (not used): Redfearn.

<<<◇>>>

Saturday, February 10th, 1990
Latics 2 (Palmer, Ritchie), Stoke City 0

Back on song

Having been distracted by their cup exploits, Latics got their promotion bid back on track with a first league victory since Boxing Day. The match proved a lack-lustre affair, though, and they were fortunate that bottom-of-the-table Stoke were of little threat as the unbeaten home run was extended to a remarkable 31 matches. Despite a below-par performance, Latics ought to have been ahead by the break as they had a number of decent chances. Scott McGarvey was replaced by Roger Palmer at the break and did not take long to make an impact, as he had also done the previous week at West Brom.

Palmer made the breakthrough in the 54th minute, firing home following a low cross from Neil Adams for his eighth goal of the campaign. Winger Adams, who had been in sparkling form for several weeks, also provided the assist for the second goal,

131

which sealed victory midway through the second period. He sprayed a pass to Denis Irwin, whose low cross from the right found Ritchie, who turned defender John Butler to score with a shot which took a slight deflection past keeper Peter Fox for his 22nd goal of the season. Latics had a host of chances in the last quarter of the match and ought to have triumphed by a more comfortable margin. But, after a succession of draws, they were simply happy to be back to winning ways in the Second Division.

LATICS: Hallworth, Irwin, Barlow, Henry, Marshall, Barrett, Adams, Ritchie, McGarvey (Palmer 46), Milligan, R Holden. Sub (not used): Redfearn.

<<<<>>>>

Saturday, February 24th, 1990
Latics 4 (Marshall 2, Palmer, Irwin), Ipswich Town 1 (Wark)

Promotion priority

Latics put their energy-sapping exploits in two cup competitions behind them to register an emphatic victory against Ipswich. Despite the pursuit of a Wembley place in both the Littlewoods Cup and FA Cup, manager Joe Royle had once again reiterated that promotion remained the main objective for the 1989/90 campaign. And the players remained focused to post a win which kept them flying high in fourth place and still within range of second-placed Sheffield United. At the same time, though, leaders Leeds appeared out of reach because they stood 10 points clear of Royle's team.

The atmosphere was described as somewhat flat, which was probably no surprise in the aftermath of the heady cup nights at Boundary Park. Once Ian Marshall, Latics' new goalscoring hero, broke the deadlock in the 38th minute with a drive from the edge of the penalty area, there was no way back for the Suffolk side. Marshall was revelling in his new role in the absence of the injured Frank Bunn and Andy Ritchie, having also scored in the FA Cup fifth-round replay at Everton three days earlier. He was on the mark again two minutes later, heading home a Rick Holden cross to leave Ipswich with an uphill battle.

Latics would have been much further ahead but for the heroics of Ipswich keeper Craig Forrest, who made a number of important saves. Marshall turned provider for Latics' third goal early in the second half as a neat flick released Roger Palmer, who coolly lobbed Forrest. John Wark pulled a goal back for Ipswich before Denis Irwin restored the three-goal advantage in the 73th minute. The defender gained possession following an interception and exchanged passes with Marshall before bursting into the box to fire home a low, left-foot drive.

LATICS: Hallworth, Irwin, Barlow, Henry, Warhurst, Barrett, Adams, Palmer, Marshall (McGarvey 80), Milligan, R Holden. Sub (not used): Redfearn.

<<<<>>>

Saturday, March 3rd, 1990
Brighton & Hove Albion 1 (Gotsmanov), Latics 1 (Adams)

Adams super strike

Lucky Latics escaped with a point following a performance described by manager Joe Royle as their worst of the season. They extended their unbeaten run to 11 matches and maintained their momentum thanks to a spectacular 35-yard equaliser from substitute Neil Adams. There was no disguising the displeasure of Royle, who remarked: "Neil scored one of the goals of the season, but it did not belong in a game like that. We were poor and that was our worst display by a long way this season. Without being disrespectful to Brighton, we have to win games like that if we want to go up." Not even the return of 25-goal Andy Ritchie after a two-match absence through injury could provide the sparkle which was sadly lacking. Ritchie had little to cheer as he even missed a penalty which would have given Latics the lead. Had Ritchie, who was fouled by Keith Dublin, scored from the spot midway through the opening period, he would have extended his club record by finding the net for a ninth successive match.

Brighton, the more dangerous team, made the breakthrough nine minutes into the second half with a debut goal from Russian Serge Gotsmanov, who shot across keeper Jon Hallworth from a tight angle. The striker, who had once scored for Russia against England at Wembley, was beginning a one-month trial at the Goldstone Ground. Royle's response was to substitute defender Paul Warhurst, send on winger Adams and once more go with three at the back. And yet again his Midas touch was in evidence as Adams scored a goal out of nothing with a 35-yard drive which gave Seagulls keeper John Keeley no hope. Not surprisingly, Adams described it as the sort of goal a player scores only once in their career. Sadly, the strike failed to spark Latics to life and they rarely looked like stepping up another gear and taking maximum points.

LATICS: Hallworth, Irwin, Barlow, Henry, Warhurst (Adams 57), Barrett, Palmer, Ritchie, Marshall, Milligan, R Holden. Sub (not used): Redfearn.

<<<<>>>>

Saturday, March 17th, 1990
Barnsley 1 (Milligan og), Latics 0

Champagne flat

Joe Royle's pre-match warning that it could be difficult to keep his players grounded after their cup exploits came home to roost with their defeat at lowly Barnsley. "We've spent more time drinking champagne than we have been training. It's been a remarkable season," he explained. The Chronicle's Bob Young pointed out that Latics could kiss goodbye to automatic promotion if they allowed poor teams like Barnsley to beat them. He believed Latics had proved they had the ability to grace the First Division, but questioned whether they had the qualities to scrap and scrape their way out of a minefield of mediocrity at their level. The greater the expectation, he added, the greater the disappointment as it now looked as though Latics would have to direct their energies towards clinching promotion through the play-offs. If the defeat proved anything, he argued, it was that Latics were mortal. He also explained that no matter how good your team are or how poor the opposition, if your luck is not in, it is not in.

At Oakwell, where Latics had a 4,000 following, the side were well on top until Barnsley scored their 'fluke' winner against the run of play mid-way through the opening half. From a corner, the ball skimmed off the head of striker Steve Cooper and went into the net off the unlucky Mike Milligan. Yet had Latics, still without the injured Frank Bunn and Andy Ritchie, taken their first-half chances, they could have easily established a 5-1 advantage. Ian Marshall, the stand-in striker who had been on a red-hot scoring spree, might well have had a first-half hat-trick while numerous other opportunities went begging. Not even Royle's decision to introduce substitute Neil Adams early in the second half and go back to his back-up plan of using three defenders, worked this time. However, if Latics had enjoyed even a slice of fortune, they would have left with at least one point rather than slip out of the top six for the first time in several months.

LATICS: Hallworth, Irwin, Barlow, Henry, Barrett, Warhurst (Adams 52), Redfearn, Palmer, Marshall, Milligan, R Holden. Sub (not used): Williams.

<<<<<>>>>

Tuesday, March 20th, 1990
Latics 4 (Palmer 2, Redfearn, Milligan), Bournemouth 0

Watching brief

Latics gave new £225,000 club-record signing Paul Moulden an exciting glimpse of Boundary Park life as he looked on. They put four goals past Bournemouth despite being without strikers Frank Bunn and Andy Ritchie – a state of affairs which underlined the scale of Moulden's challenge to hold down a regular first-team place. Latics provided the perfect riposte to criticisms which followed their defeat at Barnsley three days earlier. There was to be no mistake this time as they produced a feast of attacking football to revive their hopes of landing a promotion play-off place.

Latics made the breakthrough after 14 minutes when Neil Redfearn scored from close range after Ian Marshall headed a Paul Warhurst cross towards goal. They ought to have built on that advantage as Nick Henry, Roger Palmer, Earl Barrett, Redfearn and Rick Holden all had clear-cut chances in a one-sided opening half. They needed the cushion of a second goal and it came straight from the restart when Mike Milligan scored at the right end, firing home a rebound after Marshall's initial effort was blocked. It was now a case of how many Latics would win by as they carved open the visiting defence with ease. Palmer helped himself to two goals to increase his total for the season to 14. Barrett created his first with a precision pass and Holden provided the assist for the second with an inch-perfect cross for him to head home. With two further home games to follow in quick succession, Latics were again within striking distance of a top-six spot.

LATICS: Hallworth, Irwin, Barlow, Henry (Adams 45), Barrett, Warhurst, Redfearn, Palmer, Marshall, Milligan, R Holden. Sub (not used): Williams.

'PINCH ME NOT'

Saturday, March 24th, 1990
Latics 3 (Palmer 2, Marshall), Hull City 2 (Hunter, Jobson)

Top-two target

Suddenly, the talk was not just of the play-offs but of Latics going straight up as a second successive home win propelled them back into the top six. They were only six points behind second-placed Sheffield United with a game in hand, so their hopes of automatic promotion were rekindled. And the key figure in the upturn in fortunes was Roger Palmer, who scored twice for the second consecutive match.

The club's all-time leading scorer was clearly in no mood to relinquish his place, with Frank Bunn, Andy Ritchie and record signing Paul Moulden all on the sidelines. Palmer, 31, had been with Latics for more than a decade, but showed he had lost none of his zest as he took his season's tally to 16. It was just as well he was on top of his game as the struggling Tigers proved stubborn opponents. His goals around the half-hour, both clinically converted, appeared to put Latics in the driving seat and they looked home and dry early in the second half when Palmer turned provider to set up Ian Marshall for the third. But Hull displayed spirit to mount a comeback that saw Paul Hunter and Richard Jobson pull back goals and set the scene for an anxious final 15 minutes in which the visitors pressed for an equaliser. In the end, a victory which at one stage looked like being a rout was a hard-fought one, though winning remained the priority at this important stage of the season.

LATICS: Hallworth, Irwin, Barlow, Henry, Barrett, Warhurst, Redfearn, Palmer, Marshall, Milligan (Adams 53), R Holden. Sub (not used): Moulden.

Wednesday, March 28th, 1990
Latics 0, Sheffield United 2 (Deane 2)

Home run ends

As soon as Latics' hopes of an automatic promotion place soared, they were effectively ended by this first defeat at Boundary Park for 14 months. It was a case of the 39th step proving one too many as promotion rivals Sheffield United strengthened their hold on second spot. It was also the first time Latics had failed to score at home in 39 matches since they lost 1-0 against Manchester City. Though they remained in a play-off spot, Royle's men now found themselves nine points behind the Blades with 11 league matches left – a massive mountain to scale if they were to finish in the top two. It was not for the lack of effort as Latics laid siege to the visitors' goal in the second period and played with five forwards for the final half hour, but were unable to cut a way through.

It might well have been a happier outcome had Ian Marshall not missed a penalty early in the second half when it was 1-0. Latics were hustled and harried out of their stride by the no-frills, direct approach of the Blades, who took the lead on the half hour when an Ian Bryson corner was not cleared, leaving Brian Deane to score from close range. It was an altogether different story after the interval, with Roger Palmer striking an upright and Marshall winning a penalty by being shoved off the ball. When keeper Simon Tracey saved the spot-kick, though, the feeling that it was not going to be their day was reinforced. Royle sent on Neil Adams and the debutant Paul Moulden to try and provide more attacking bite. But the Blades sealed victory with 12 minutes left when a long clearance from Tracey was flicked on by Bryson for Deane to lob keeper Jon Hallworth.

LATICS: Hallworth, Irwin, Barlow (Adams 57), Henry, Barrett, Warhurst, Redfearn (Moulden 57), Palmer, Marshall, Milligan, R Holden.

<<<<>>>>

Saturday, March 31st, 1990
Middlesbrough 1 (Slaven), Latics 0

Teesside torment

Latics' push for promotion was described as grinding to a halt following their latest defeat on the road. It was another case of the away-day blues and proving a major handicap to their hopes of a top-six finish. More precisely, it was a season-long shortage of goals on the road which was holding Latics back. They had found the net only 15 times in 17 away league matches and had scored just 21 goals in 23 games in all competitions on their travels. The absence of the injured Andy Ritchie was pinpointed as one significant factor. It proved a mystifying problem because the side were generally performing well on their trips and lacking only a cutting edge. With six of their final 10 league matches away, it was observed that these games would determine whether the league season ended in glory or disappointment.

The only cheer for Latics at Ayresome Park were the long-awaited returns of Frank Bunn and Andy Holden after lay-offs of three and seven months respectively, while Andy Rhodes was preferred to Jon Hallworth. It was the keeper's first recall since being dropped for the New Year's Day match at Leeds. The only goal came after 26 minutes when Latics failed to clear a corner and Ian Baird set up Bernie Slaven, who scored his 27th of the campaign. How Latics could have done with such a predator in front of goal as they again dominated lengthy periods without having anything to show for their efforts. Their cause was not helped by the loss of Rick Holden late in the opening period with a recurrence of a foot injury that resulted in Roger Palmer being moved to the right flank. Neil Redfearn switched to the left as Paul Moulden went on partner Frank Bunn up front. And, midway through the second half, manager Joe Royle took off Redfearn and employed defender Paul Warhurst as a central striker to try and find a route to goal. It was substitutes Warhurst and Moulden who had the best chances of rescuing a point when Boro keeper Stephen Pears made a fabulous double save to deny them.

LATICS: Rhodes, Irwin, Barlow, Henry, Barrett, A Holden, Redfearn (Warhurst 67), Palmer, Bunn, Milligan, R Holden (Moulden 43).

<<<<>>>>

Tuesday, April 3rd, 1990
Leicester City 3 (Kelly 2, North), Latics 0

Form falters

Latics completed an unwanted hat-trick with a third successive league loss. Having blown their hopes of automatic promotion, this was hardly the ideal preparation for their FA Cup semi-final against Manchester United five days' later. Captain Mike Milligan remained convinced, however, that Latics would overcome their worrying dip in form. "Everyone is a bit down at the moment because we are not getting the breaks in front of goal," he said. "But, by the time Sunday comes round, we'll be raring to go again and we'll bounce back. There are still nine games to go in the

Second Division and our main priority is promotion. I still think it is still a possibility. We have certainly not given up yet."

Latics didn't deserve to lose 3-0 on the balance of play. Yet again, though, they were punished for defensive errors while once more being unable to take the chances they created. This was the third successive game in which they had failed to hit the target and they were up against it from the 12th minute when Marc North gave Leicester the lead. It could have been even worse soon afterwards but for Andy Barlow's goal-line clearance to keep out a header from Steve Walsh. It was far from one-sided, however, and Latics would have been level by the break but for two superb saves from Martin Hodge to deny Andy Ritchie and Paul Moulden. Leicester doubled their advantage shortly after the restart through David Kelly, who slotted home after Andy Rhodes had made a marvellous reaction save to keep out his initial effort. The Foxes sealed victory midway through the half when Kelly struck for a second time after former Latics winger Tommy Wright cut the ball back from the left wing. For Kelly, it must have felt like sweet revenge because, not long before, he had been in the West Ham team who lost 6-0 at Boundary Park in the semi-finals of the Littlewoods Cup.

LATICS: Rhodes, Irwin, Barlow, Henry (Palmer 60), Barrett, A Holden, Redfearn, Ritchie, Marshall, Milligan, Moulden. Sub (not used): Warhurst.

Friday, April 13th, 1990
Latics 3 (Holden 2, Bunn), Leeds United 1 (Davison)

Lucky thirteen

There was nothing unlucky for Latics with the date of this game as they defeated Second Division leaders Leeds United for a third time in the campaign. It was their fourth meeting of the season and Latics made it three wins and one draw. They must have wished they could play Leeds every week! After four straight defeats, they showed great resilience as the match took place only 38 hours after the FA Cup loss against Manchester United. It was just the sort of game they needed to pick themselves up after the semi-final and such was the importance of the match that the noon kick-off was delayed by 15 minutes because of crowd congestion.

Latics broke the deadlock midway through the opening half when Leeds conceded a penalty for a foul on Mike Milligan. Rick Holden stepped forward to score from the spot. Frank Bunn headed against the bar and had another effort well saved as Latics had to wait until the middle of the second period before doubling their advantage when Holden struck again after a goalmouth melee. They clinched victory in the 72nd minute when substitute Neil Redfearn set up Bunn, who sprinted clear to chip keeper Mervyn Day from outside the penalty area. Bobby Davison scored a consolation goal for Leeds, but Latics ought to have restored their three-goal advantage when Holden missed a great chance to complete his hat-trick.

LATICS: Hallworth, Irwin, Barlow, Henry, Barrett, Warhurst, Adams (Redfearn 58), Moulden (Ritchie 81), Bunn, Milligan, R Holden.

<<<◇>>>

Monday, April 16th, 1990
Port Vale 2 (Beckford 2), Latics 0

Beckford's ball

Latics' promotion hopes were dealt another setback with their Easter Monday defeat in the Potteries. Unless they could rediscover the elusive goal touch on their travels, the chances of them making the play-offs looked remote. Once more, it was not a case of them playing badly in an away match, but the stark fact was that they had not managed a league goal on the road in four trips. In fact, a total of 15 goals in 19 away games was desperately disappointing for a side with such a positive approach to their football. Only Stoke, who were already relegated, had a worse away goal-scoring record. More clinical finishing on the road would have given Latics enough points to have been in the top two, let alone be scrambling for a play-off berth. Even 26-goal top scorer Andy Ritchie seemed to be finding goals hard to come by as he had scored only three away from Boundary Park, and one of those was a penalty.

He could easily have doubled his away goals tally as he had six clear-cut chances while Neil Redfearn and Earl Barrett also went close. But Vale snatched the lead five minutes before the break when Darren Beckford stole ahead of Barrett at the near post to slot home a low centre from Nicky Cross. And, five minutes after the restart, the visitors' defence was undone again from a Ray Walker free-kick as Beckford, who would later become a Latics player, struck his seventh goal in as many games and 19th for the season. Latics enjoyed long periods of possession and even gambled with five up front, but still they could not find the net. The defeat left them seven points adrift of the play-off places, though they had played three fewer matches than the teams above them.

LATICS: Hallworth, Irwin, Barlow, Henry, Barrett, Warhurst (Palmer 20), Redfearn, Ritchie, Bunn, Moulden (Adams 50), R Holden.

<<<<>>>>

Wednesday, April 18th, 1990
Plymouth Argyle 2 (McCarthy 2), Latics 0

McCarthy magic

Two first-half goals from Sean McCarthy, another striker who would later move to Boundary Park, inflicted a further blow to Latics' fading promotion hopes. The defeat left them seven points behind sixth-placed Sunderland, albeit with two matches in hand, and a frustrated Joe Royle said: "I did not think we were that bad, but we cannot keep giving sides a two-goal start. We are making individual errors and paying the penalty for them. We are continually losing to sides who are not as good as us. I do not mean that disrespectfully to Plymouth, but we can't go on giving away silly goals."

Latics fell behind in the 18th minute following a mistake by Paul Warhurst which allowed McCarthy to break clear and shoot past keeper Jon Hallworth. McCarthy doubled Plymouth's advantage on the stroke of half-time with a far-post header that continued his spectacular upturn in form. He had scored only five goals in 24 league games up to Easter, but, over the holiday weekend, also scored a hat-trick at West Brom to make it five goals in two matches. Royle sent on Neil Adams for Warhurst at the break and went with an adventurous 3-3-4 formation, but the bold move still failed to muster the goal that could have opened the game up. In the second half, luck deserted Latics as Neil Redfearn struck the woodwork while Roger Palmer and Andy Ritchie were both denied by superb saves from keeper Rhys Wilmot. The two wins pulled Plymouth clear of the relegation places, but Latics' hopes of a top-six finish were dealt another setback.

'PINCH ME NOT'

LATICS: Hallworth, Irwin, Barlow, Henry, Barrett, Warhurst (Adams 46), Redfearn, Ritchie, Bunn, Palmer, R Holden. Sub (not used): Moulden.

<<<◇>>>

Saturday, April 21st, 1990
Latics 3 (Ritchie, Bunn 2), West Ham United 0

Front-two reunited

Frank Bunn's return to fitness and form came at just the right time for Latics in their quest for end-of-season honours. The striker, who had been out for three months from the turn of the year following knee surgery, scored twice to make it three goals in four matches following his return. Bunn's on-field partnership with Ritchie had been a significant factor for Latics in the recent seasons but, for large chunks of this campaign, they had been split up by injury. They shared the goals as Latics inflicted

MR RELIABLE....Andy Barlow played in 63 of Latics' 65 matches during the 'pinch-me season.'

more pain and misery on the Hammers following their triumph over them in the semi-final of the Littlewoods Cup. Their heroics also revived the side's hopes of a top-six spot, though West Ham, with Billy Bonds in charge, showed more steel than they had earlier under Lou Macari when they were beaten 6-0 at Boundary Park.

The visitors took no prisoners in what was described as a scruffy, scrappy first half in which the highlight was Rick Holden teasing and tormenting Hammers' right-back George Parris. Latics had to be patient in waiting until the 52nd minute to make a breakthrough when Neil

142

Redfearn was tripped by keeper Ludek Miklosko and Ritchie blasted home from the penalty spot for his 27th goal of the season. Three minutes later and it was 2-0 when Bunn slotted home a Denis Irwin pull-back from an Andy Barlow cross. Latics were playing their 59th game of the season, but it was West Ham who wilted late on as Mike Milligan stormed forward from midfield and released Bunn, who made no mistake with a shot from 10 yards. This was only Latics' second win in seven league matches and it lifted Boundary Park spirits considerably.

LATICS: Rhodes, Irwin, Barlow, Henry, Barrett, Warhurst, Redfearn, Ritchie, Bunn, Milligan, R Holden. Subs (not used): Palmer, Adams.

Tuesday, April 24th, 1990
Portsmouth 2 (Wigley, Chamberlain), Latics 1 (Barrett)

Dirty dozen

This wasn't an ideal Wembley warm-up as Latics suffered a sixth successive away league defeat. It seemed one loss too many, with hopes of a play-off place massively hit. Latics were left in ninth place, five points adrift of sixth-placed Sunderland, with only four league fixtures remaining. It was now going to take a super-human effort to reach the top six, though captain Mike Milligan refused to concede defeat. "Two of our games are against Wolves and Sunderland, who are also battling for play-off places, so I have not given up hope," he declared. The loss at Fratton Park was Latics' 12th on their league travels, their last success coming at West Ham in mid-December. That was the reason they would ultimately fail to reach the play-offs.

Latics could have no complaints about the loss and, but for the heroics of keeper Andy Rhodes, would have been defeated by a much heavier margin. After an opening half hour which was described as a non-event, Latics went ahead when Earl Barrett headed home a Neil Redfearn corner. Barrett, who was badly concussed, continued after a lengthy stoppage, but was replaced at half-time by Paul Warhurst. Six minutes after the opener, Pompey were 2-1 ahead following strikes from Steve Wigley and Mark Chamberlain as the visitors capitulated. Rhodes then pulled off great saves to deny Guy Whittingham, Chamberlain and substitute Jimmy Gilligan late on.

LATICS: Rhodes, Irwin, Barlow, Henry (Palmer 46), A Holden, Barrett (Warhurst 46), Redfearn, Ritchie, Bunn, Milligan, R Holden.

Tuesday, May 1st, 1990
Latics 4 (R Holden 3, Palmer), Oxford United 1 (Ford)

Holden's heroics

Rick Holden hit a fine hat-trick two days after the Wembley disappointment to help destroy Oxford. It was a measure of the team's character that they came out fighting in an irrepressible display. Reaching the play-offs was still looking a huge challenge, however, following Sunderland's win at Port Vale. That effectively meant Latics had to win their last three matches, including one at Roker Park.

The crowd of 12,616 gave the team a rapturous reception on their homecoming after Wembley. The Chaddy End was packed to capacity, so hundreds of fans were redirected to the Rochdale Road End. Oxford were on the retreat from the start and the only surprise was that the breakthrough took 37 minutes. The wingers combined perfectly as Neil Adams crossed for Holden to find the net with a looping header. Holden was on target again in the 50th minute after Andy Ritchie beat the offside trap before crossing for him to pop up at the near post and force the ball home.

Paul Moulden supplied the assist for Roger Palmer to score the third with seven minutes left. There was a flurry of late activity as Mike Ford pulled one back before Holden fittingly had the last word in stoppage time. Paul Warhurst made a blistering break out of defence and released Holden, who cut in from the left to net with a smartly-struck shot for his 13th goal of the season. Repeat performances in the three remaining matches were still required to keep the promotion dream alive.

LATICS: Rhodes, Donachie, Barlow, Palmer, Barrett, Warhurst, Adams, Ritchie (Redfearn 71), Bunn (Moulden 79), Milligan, R Holden.

Thursday, May 3rd, 1990
Latics 1 (Palmer), Wolverhampton Wanderers 1 (Steele)

Steele shocker

Hopes of promotion all but died in the cruellest of ways as substitute Tim Steele scored an 87th minute equaliser for Wolves. It looked as though the goal of a top-six finish would still be a possibility after Roger Palmer had given Latics a first-half lead.

But the odds would still have been stacked heavily against them, with the need to win their last two matches – both away – as well as relying on Blackburn and Swindon losing. And, as the Latics players made a tearful lap of honour following their final home match of the season, they were left to reflect on a disappointing month. There had been defeats in the semi-finals of the FA Cup and the final of the Littlewoods Cup as well as a nosedive in their promotion bid.

Manager Joe Royle wasn't conceding defeat, though deep down he must have known their season had petered out. "We have got to keep trying. We'll turn up at Sunderland and Bradford and give it a go," he said defiantly. Royle added that Latics had not missed out on promotion because of the draw against Wolves, but through events in the preceding 43 league matches. They had lost 13 times, 12 of them on their travels. "I have my own theories as to why that should be and we'll be making every effort to rectify the problem," he explained. Wolves were far more robust opponents than Oxford 48 hours earlier and Latics were not helped by the injury-enforced absences of Denis Irwin, Nick Henry, Ian Marshall and Andy Holden.

Without the physical presence of Marshall and Holden, Steve Bull ran amok and could have scored a first half hat-trick, keeper Andy Rhodes making a couple of fabulous saves.

It was against the run of play that Latics took a 39th minute lead when Palmer crashed home his 19th goal of the season. Another injury blow hit them when they lost midfield man Mike Milligan at the break with a shoulder injury. But they made light of the absence of their captain and began the second period strongly as substitute Frank Bunn had an effort cleared off the line by Paul Cook and saw another strike the bar. Just when it appeared Latics had secured victory, along came crushing disappointment

Draw leaves Oldham with paper-thin hopes

By Ian Ross

Oldham Athletic............ 1
Wolves 1

OLDHAM Athletic's dream of climaxing the club's most successful season by returning to the first division for the first time since 1923 lives on, but only just.

At Boundary Park last night, Oldham, the beaten Littlewoods Cup finalists who were playing the 63rd game of an extraordinary campaign, were outplayed by a spirited Wolverhampton Wanderers, yet still managed to collect a point that keeps alive their play-off hopes.

If Oldham defeat Sunderland at Roker Park tomorrow and Bradford City at Valley Parade on Monday, they may achieve a place in the top six of the second division.

Despite the resilience of players who are suffering from fatigue, it is, however, a tall order. Oldham last won a game away from home almost five months ago.

The goal which denied them a crucial victory came two min-

utes before the final whistle when Steele, a second-half substitute, swept home a Downing cross from close range.

Oldham's early play was so erratic and uncoordinated that they might have welcomed the abandonment of the fixture by the fifteenth minute.

Wolves, whose own chances of reaching the play-offs evaporated last week, used the predictable ploy of pumping the ball into their opponents' half of the field, an area within which Bull, the England international forward, invariably lurked. It nearly succeeded.

On a better day, when his timing was good rather than adequate, Bull would have claimed a treble before the

Top of second division

	P	W	D	L	F	A	Pts
Leeds Utd	45	23	13	9	78	52	82
Sheff Utd	45	23	13	9	73	56	82
Newcastle	45	22	14	9	79	51	80
Sunderland	45	20	14	11	68	61	74
Swindon	45	20	13	12	78	58	73
Blackburn	45	19	16	10	73	58	73
West Ham	45	19	12	14	76	57	69
Oldham	44	18	13	13	66	54	67
Wolves	45	18	13	14	67	56	67
Ipswich	45	18	12	15	64	65	66

interval. He would have scored as early as the nineteenth second had Rhodes, the Oldham goalkeeper, not dived to turn aside a close-range shot.

Bull squandered five more inviting chances as below-par Oldham were overrun by a side that adapted to the synthetic surface with uncommon ease. As if to prove that football can still be the cruellest sport, Oldham took an undeserved lead after 39 minutes when Palmer stabbed home from 12 yards after Donachie had flicked on a corner.

Despite losing the influential Milligan during the interval, Oldham performed with a good deal more poise in the second half. Yet Bull was still posing a constant threat as Wolves continued to impress until they entered the final third of the field, where the cultured Barrett excelled.

OLDHAM ATHLETIC: A Rhodes; W Donachie, A Barlow, N Redfearn, E Barrett, P Warhurst, N Adams, A Ritchie, R Palmer, M Milligan (sub: F Bunn), R Holden.

WOLVERHAMPTON WANDERERS: M Kendall, T Bennett, A Thompson, M Venus, S Westley, G Bellamy, P Cook, K Downing, S Bull, J Paskin, R Dennison (sub: J Steele).

Referee: J Key.

after Paul Warhurst delayed a clearance. Bull, who was shortly to depart to Italy for World Cup finals duty with England, picked up the loose ball and released Cook, whose cross was steered home by Steele, leaving Latics little time to repair the damage. Many of the players left the field in tears, realising they had blown their promotion hopes. But they re-emerged to take a well-deserved lap of honour when the tremendous ovation they received was a heartfelt thank-you to the players for this once-in-a-lifetime campaign.

LATICS: Rhodes, Donachie, Barlow, Redfearn, Barrett, Warhurst, Adams, Ritchie, Palmer, Milligan (Bunn 46), R Holden. Sub (not used): Moulden.

<<<<>>>>

Saturday, May 5th, 1990
Sunderland 2 (Owers, Armstrong), Latics 3 (Adams, Ritchie, Palmer)

Too little, too late

What a pity Latics left it so late in the season to finally make an impact on their travels! If their efforts at Sunderland and Bradford over the Bank Holiday weekend could have been evident a few times earlier in the season, they would not have missed on the promotion play-offs. Four goals and four points from their final two fixtures were not enough to earn any tangible reward for their memorable 65-game campaign. Latics could still have sneaked into the top six when they kicked off at Roker Park, though they needed to beat Sunderland and rely on Blackburn and Swindon losing. Both of those sides drew their final league matches. In the end, Latics missed out on a top-six spot by three points despite finishing the season with a team decimated by injuries.

Sunderland manager Denis Smith, whose side were assured of a play-off place, paid tribute to Latics, describing them as 'probably the best team in the Second Division.' "They have been magnificent. They have been a credit to the division and a great advert for football," he said. Latics were less cavalier without the injured Ian Marshall, Andy Holden, Denis Irwin, Mike Milligan, Nick Henry and Frank Bunn while Paul Warhurst limped off in the opening half with a hamstring strain. It was very much a patched-up side with the depleted back four comprising Willie Donachie and Gary Williams at full-back and Earl Barrett and Andy Barlow as the central-defensive pairing.

Latics drew first blood after 26 minutes through a looping header from Neil Adams, only for Gary Owers to equalise when he reacted quickly after his initial effort had come back off the crossbar. And the only reason the opening half finished at 1-1 was because of a penalty save by Andy Rhodes from Paul Hardyman. Latics displayed all their battling qualities after the interval to establish a commanding 3-1 lead through strikes from Andy Ritchie and Roger Palmer before Gordon Armstrong pulled a goal back for Sunderland in the dying minutes. But the midfielder could not prevent Latics winning for only the fourth time on their arduous 1989-90 league travels.

LATICS: Rhodes, Donachie, Barlow, Redfearn, Barrett, Warhurst (Williams 38), Adams, Ritchie, Palmer, Moulden, R Holden. Sub (not used): McGarvey.

<<<<>>>>

Monday, May 7th, 1990
Bradford City 1 (Adcock), Latics 1 (Redfearn)

Fans' farewell

It was a measure of what an incredible season Latics had that they took over 2,000 fans to West Yorkshire, even though they had blown their promotion hopes. Bradford were already relegated and Latics had around one third of the crowd of 6,798 for what was a meaningless match. The opening half was goalless, Gary Williams and Paul Moulden having clear-cut chances for Latics, whose keeper Andy Rhodes made a superb save to deny Neil Woods. Paul Jewell had three chances for Bradford early in the second half as Latics lived dangerously.

Latics, who also had their moments, made the breakthrough shortly after the hour mark when Willie Donachie's shot was blocked and rebounded for Neil Redfearn to rifle home. Bradford equalised nine minutes later when Tony Adcock raced clear on to a pass from Mark Aizlewood to fire home. Rhodes saved well from Adcock and Jewell late on to preserve the point whereas Moulden and Roger Palmer might have won it for Latics. But, as the team trooped off the field for the 65th and final time, they were left to reflect on a campaign which will go down as possibly the most remarkable in the club's history, even though it turned out to be an "if only" season in which they were cruelly left empty-handed.

LATICS: Rhodes, Donachie, Barlow, Redfearn, Barrett, Williams, Adams, Ritchie, Palmer, Moulden, R Holden. Subs (not used): McGarvey, Makin.

<<<<>>>

MISCELLANY

Tuesday, November 28th, 1989
Zenith Data Systems Cup, second round
Newcastle United 2 (Quinn 2), Latics 0

The tie from 1989/90 most people have forgotten is the one Latics lost at St James' Park in the Zenith Data Systems Cup. Just as in the earlier league game there, Latics' old-boy Mick Quinn was the architect of their downfall, scoring both goals. Though it was still only November, he had 19 goals in the season and prompted Joe Royle to declare: "If he was playing five-a-side on another planet, he would still score."

Royle was without five regulars, an indication as to how highly the competition rated in his priorities. The line-up included squad players Willie Donachie, Gary Williams and Scott McGarvey, along with teenage left-back Chris Blundell. Another youngster, Norman Kelly, was on the bench. Newcastle took the lead after only four minutes when Quinn headed home John Gallacher's cross. And Latics' woes deepened when Mike Milligan limped off with a groin strain. Quinn sealed victory with two minutes left with a near-post shot from a Wayne Fereday cross.

LATICS: Rhodes, Irwin, Blundell, Donachie, Barrett, Williams, Adams, Ritchie, McGarvey, Milligan (Palmer 19), R Holden (Kelly 55).

APPEARANCES

The ever-reliable Earl Barrett appeared in all 65 of Latics' league and cup games during their marathon campaign. Indeed, there were seven players who featured in 60 or more matches, an indication as to how settled a side they had. The full list of appearances, with substitute outings in brackets, was: Barrett 65, R Holden 64, Barlow 61 (2), Irwin 60, Milligan 60, Henry 58 (2), Ritchie 50 (1), Palmer 44 (18), Marshall 37 (3), Rhodes 36 (1), Warhurst 36 (10), Bunn 34 (1), Adams 30 (18), Hallworth 29, Redfearn 20, Donachie 8, A Holden 8, McGarvey 6 (12), Moulden 5, Williams 2 (25), Heseltine 1 (5), Blundell 1, Kelly (1), Mooney (1), Makin (1).

GOALSCORERS

Latics found the net 110 times in their 65 games, with Andy Ritchie heading the scoring chart with 28 goals. And, but for a month-long absence through injury, he would surely have reached 30. It was a measure of how the goals were spread that four players reached double figures for the season. The full list of goalscorers was: Ritchie 28, Palmer 20, Bunn 13, R Holden 13, Milligan 8, Marshall 6, Adams 5, Barrett 4, Redfearn 3, McGarvey 2, Barlow 1, Henry 1, Irwin 1, Warhurst 1, own goals 4.

ATTENDANCES

Crowd figures at Boundary Park were their highest for more than a decade as the cup exploits captured the public imagination. Home league crowds were up by almost 30 per cent at 222,151 for the 23 matches, an average of 9,659. That was compared with 165,650 for the 1988/89 campaign, in which the average was 7,202. In total, Latics had 370,910 spectators at their 33 home games, at an average of 11,240. Taking into account the 74,343 crowd at Wembley and 79,031 who attended the two FA Cup semi-finals against Manchester United, Latics were seen live by almost one million people.

Diary of the season

MAY

1: Andy Barlow and Andy Rhodes, who went on to become key members of the 1989/90 team, submitted transfer requests after both were unhappy at being unable to hold down regular first-team places.

2: Long-serving defender Gary Hoolickin (31) lost a two-year battle to overcome a serious knee injury and announced his retirement after 15 years at Oldham.

9: Having sold strikers Mike Cecere to Huddersfield and Tony Philliskirk to Preston for £60,000 and £50,000 respectively, Joe Royle splashed out £22,000 to Bristol City for Scott McGarvey to provide extra firepower.

11: Latics announced plans to install a £50,000 scoreboard at Boundary Park which, at 54ft 7in by 10ft 8in, would be the third-largest in the land behind Wembley and St James' Park, Newcastle.

25: Ten apprentices were signed up, including Chris Makin, Paul Gerrard and Paul Bernard, all three of

MAY SIGNING.......Paul Bernard.

whom would go on to become first-team and international players while at Boundary Park.

29: A three-year deal with North-West construction firm Ashdene and Windsor, who took over the sponsorship of the main stand from Weatherseal, could earn Latics as much as £100,000 depending on success on the pitch.

31: Winger Tommy Wright (23) rejected the offer of a new four-year contract, citing a burning desire to play in the First Division.

JUNE

5: Perimeter fencing was removed from the members-only areas in front of the main and Broadway stands – a move which had been planned before the Hillsborough tragedy a couple of months earlier. There were no plans to remove the fences from behind both goals.

11: Winger Neil Adams, who had a two-month loan spell at Boundary Park earlier in the year, completed a £100,000 move from Everton as Latics beat off competition from Barnsley and Notts County. It was viewed as a significant move, bearing in mind Wright's desire to leave.

12: Hull made an inquiry for transfer-listed defender Peter Skipper, who had lost his place in January after Andy Holden was captured from Wigan in a £130,000 deal.

14: Latics landed a three-year shirt sponsorship deal with Bovis Urban Renewal which netted them £125,000.

16: Fourth Division Scunthorpe joined the chase for Skipper, later agreeing a £35,000 fee.

21: Terry Cale, financial controller at building supplies firm Crossley Ferguson for the previous 13 years, was appointed new Latics secretary.
Peter Skipper opened transfer talks with Third Division Walsall.

'PINCH ME NOT'

JULY

4: The Skipper saga finally ended when he completed a £30,000 transfer to Walsall, agreeing a two-year contract.

9: Joe Royle slammed newspaper reports linking Denis Irwin with a £500,000 move to Manchester City.

11: Club captain John Kelly was placed on the transfer list five days before the start of pre-season training.

31: Kelly joined Skipper at Walsall after finalising a £35,000 move. He had also had talks with Shrewsbury. Andy Holden took over from Kelly as Latics' club captain.

AUGUST

1: Tommy Wright completed a £300,000 move to Leicester City, with Latics also to receive 15 per cent of any sell-on.

2: Roger Palmer scored for Latics in a 1-1 draw at Grimsby Town in the first pre-season friendly.

3: Latics called a public meeting at the Queen Elizabeth Hall, but quashed rumours they were to leave Boundary Park or merge with another club.

5: Georgian visitors Dynamo Tbilisi were beaten 4-0 at Boundary Park in a friendly, Andy Ritchie scoring twice. Roger Palmer and Neil Adams also found the net.

9: Thirteen hundred anxious fans packed into the Queen Elizabeth Hall for the public meeting to hear of plans for a £50million retail park next to Boundary Park, one which would swallow up their Little Wembley training ground. The deal involved land owned by Latics, Oldham Council and the trustees of Clayton Playing Fields. Talks had been held secretly over a six-month period.

DIARY OF THE SEASON

Strikers Frank Bunn and Andy Ritchie pledged their futures to the club by signing new four-year contracts.

10: Latics signed a two-year deal with motor group Lookers, who agreed to supply vehicles worth £41,000 each year. It was the third major sponsorship package secured in the close season.

11: Roger Palmer scored the only goal of the game as Latics completed their pre-season preparations with a 1-0 victory at Tranmere Rovers, where youth-team keeper David Wall performed heroics. Wall replaced Jon Hallworth, who went off with damaged knee ligaments – an injury which would rule him out for six weeks.

17: Forty-eight hours before the start of the season, Latics completed the £165,000 capture of Watford winger Rick Holden, a player Joe Royle had wanted to sign previously, only to find himself unable to afford the £150,000 fee when he went from Halifax to Vicarage Road.

19: A derby setback in their opening Second Division game for Latics, who lost 1-0 at Blackburn Rovers to a goal from Simon Garner.

22: Rick Holden marked his home debut with the goal which earned Latics a 1-1 draw against Watford, the team he had left less than a week earlier.

24: Midfield man Mike Milligan signed a new four-year contract to join Andy Ritchie, Frank Bunn and Ian Marshall, who had each penned similar deals.

26: Latics battled back from a 2-0 deficit to draw 2-2 against Swindon Town at Boundary Park, Roger Palmer's two goals earning an unlikely point.

AUGUST CASUALTY.....goalkeeper Jon Hallworth, who injured his knee.

153

'PINCH ME NOT'

SEPTEMBER

2: Former Latics striker Mick Quinn inflicted pain and misery on his old club as he scored both goals for Newcastle in a 2-1 win at St James' Park. Andy Holden withdrew from the Wales squad to play their World Cup qualifier in Finland with an ankle injury which would rule him out for seven months.

9: Latics recorded their first league victory of the season, at the fifth attempt, as they scraped a 3-2 home win against Plymouth Argyle.

16: Roger Palmer and Andy Ritchie scored the goals which earned Latics a 2-1 success at Stoke, the first victory on their league travels.

19: The Littlewoods Cup campaign kicked off with a 2-1 home win against Roses rivals Leeds in the first leg of their second-round tie, with Andy Ritchie and Rick Holden the goalscorers.

22: Latics decided not to pursue interest in defender Mark Talbut, son of former West Brom player John, who had been on trial from Belgian club Beerschott. They had agreed a £40,000 transfer.

23: Andy Ritchie scored twice as Latics defeated West Bromwich Albion 2-1 at Boundary Park to continue their successful run.

26: Leaders Sheffield United ended Latics' sequence of four straight wins with a 2-1 victory at Bramall Lane, where Frank Bunn scored his first goal of 1989/90.

AT THE DOUBLE .....striker Andy Ritchie, the two-goal hero against West Brom, takes aim from the penalty spot.

28: Summer-signing Scott McGarvey, unable to command a regular place, was loaned to Wigan Athletic for a month.

30: A quick return to winning ways, though Latics struggled to overcome bottom-of-the-table Leicester 1-0, courtesy of an unfortunate own goal from Simon Morgan.

OCTOBER

3: Latics knocked Leeds out of the League Cup for a third time in four seasons, completing the job they began a fortnight earlier. Goals by Frank Bunn and Andy Ritchie earned Latics a 2-1 victory at Elland Road to seal a 4-2 aggregate success.

7: Two goals in the first seven minutes from Frank Bunn and Mike Milligan set up a 2-0 home win against Barnsley in a game in which Latics were without four first-choice defenders.

9: The injury crisis forced Latics to recall defender Chris Blundell (19) from an extended loan in New Zealand.

14: Latics produced one of their worst performances of the season and were lucky to lose only 2-0 at Bournemouth.

17: Joe Royle's side gave another lack-lustre display in a goalless draw at Hull, who had now gone 23 league games without a win – the worst run in their history.

20: Teenage midfield player Norman Kelly joined Scott McGarvey on a one-month loan at Wigan.

21: Andy Ritchie scored a goal in each half as Latics comfortably defeated Middlesbrough 2-0 at Boundary Park.

24: Scott McGarvey suffered the misfortune of seeing his loan spell at Wigan cut short by a hamstring injury.

'PINCH ME NOT'

25: A memorable night for Frank Bunn, who scored a record-breaking six goals in a 7-0 demolition of Scarborough in the third round of the Littlewoods Cup.

28: Latics came from behind to earn a creditable 1-1 draw at Wolves, Mike Milligan scoring their equalising goal.

31: The comeback kings struck again as Latics twice fell behind but hit back to draw 2-2 against Bradford City and extend their unbeaten home run to 20 competitive matches over a nine-month period.

NOVEMBER

4: A useful 2-1 home victory against Sunderland, one of their promotion rivals, as Paul Warhurst opened his scoring account for Latics and Andy Ritchie also found the net.

7: Plans were announced to carry out safety work to increase the capacity in the Chaddy End by 1,000 for the Littlewoods Cup tie against Arsenal. The capacity would be 18,362 – down from 22,000 the previous season amid repercussions of the Hillsborough tragedy earlier in the year.

11: Andy Ritchie was Lord of the Manor Ground, scoring the only goal of the game against Oxford United which earned Latics their second away league victory.

18: John Keeley, who would later become a Latics player, was Brighton's goalkeeping hero as they drew 1-1 at Boundary Park in what was the snatch of the day in a match dominated by Joe Royle's side.

20: Such are Joe Royle's attacking options that 22-year-old reserve-team striker Mark Stewart was handed a free transfer.

22: Manager Joe Royle's pre-match forecast that Latics were capable of causing a Littlewoods Cup upset came true as reigning First Division champions and current league leaders Arsenal crashed to a 3-1 defeat at Boundary Park. Andy Ritchie scored twice and Nick Henry was also on target to set up a quarter-final against either Southampton or Swindon in mid-January. Cup fever hit Oldham as Latics revealed the extraordinary lengths fans pursued to get tickets for the sell-out against Arsenal. One claimed to be Manchester United chairman Martin Edwards, but, when Latics promised to send the tickets to Old Trafford, he was rumbled as he requested them to be posted to his home in Stalybridge. Another purported to be Mrs Kenny Dalglish, but the best story involved a break-in when the burglar left the video, stereo and colour television, but made off with the householder's ticket for the Arsenal match.

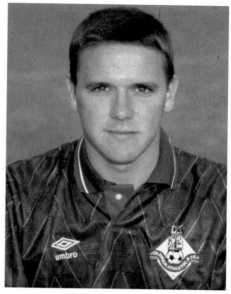

OFF THE MARK......and what a night Nick Henry chose for scoring his first goal for the club.

25: Ipswich players scored both goals in a 1-1 draw at Portman Road. Frank Yallop put the ball into his own net to give Latics the lead, only for it to be cancelled by a strike from Chris Kiwomya.

28: Latics made five changes for the Zenith Data Systems Cup-tie at Newcastle, where they lost 2-0. Frank Bunn, Nick Henry, Ian Marshall, Paul Warhurst and Andy Barlow all sat out the match.

DECEMBER

1: Latics chairman Ian Stott confirmed he was planning talks with Joe Royle in the following 24 hours after the Latics manager emerged as the favourite to take charge at Manchester City, one of his former clubs, after the sacking of Mel Machin. That same evening, Latics beat Lancashire neighbours Blackburn Rovers 2-0, Rick Holden and Andy Ritchie scoring the goals. There were emotional scenes at Boundary Park as supporters placed an advertisement on the electronic scoreboard pleading 'Please Joe, Don't Go'. They also unfurled banners displaying messages urging him to stay.

'PINCH ME NOT'

4: After a weekend of soul-searching, Royle told the Oldham Evening Chronicle he had turned down the chance to discuss a move to City and had pledged his future to Latics. Royle admitted that he had several sleepless nights, thinking long and hard about what to do before declining the chance to discuss the vacant post at Maine Road. He explained that he couldn't walk out on the club who had been dearest to his heart for seven and a half years. The manager had, in fact, pledged his immediate future to the Boundary Park club the morning after the Blackburn victory, admitting that the reaction of supporters to his possible departure tipped the balance. He said: "It was an emotional night. The fans were brilliant and you would have to be made of stone not to be influenced. City are a great club and could have offered me a short cut to the First Division, but I just could not walk away from here and leave the club in the lurch. I didn't want more than seven years of friendship with the players, staff, directors and fans to end in a way that might have left a bad taste. I had a few sleepless nights when I realised City were seriously interested in me and the interest is flattering. But I know I have made the right decision. There is a unique charm about this club which is totally different to any other I have been involved with. Not only that, but I also believe that we have a team, a unit on and off the field, that deserves First Division football, and it is my ambition to get us there. Without wanting to sound conceited, I think me going would have left the club in a very difficult position at a time when things are going well. The timing just wasn't right. I simply could not let down so many people, particularly when I have been preaching loyalty to the players and signing a lot of them on four-year contracts."

9: Royle must have wondered whether he had made the right decision as Latics lost 3-0 at Watford. It was a bizarre match in which Latics keeper Andy Rhodes was almost a spectator whereas Watford shot-stopper Tony Coton made a string of super saves.

11: Latics were paired with Third Division Birmingham City at St Andrew's in the third round of the FA Cup. Despite the cup exploits, attendances at Latics' first 10 home league matches showed a surprising seven per cent fall on the 1988/89 season. The average was 6,699 compared to 7,204 in the previous campaign.

16: Back on the road, one week after the defeat at Watford, Latics went to West Ham and recorded their third away league win. Mike Milligan scored and Colin Foster put through his own goal to seal their 2-0 triumph.

DIARY OF THE SEASON

19: Manchester United reserve-team defender Wayne Heseltine (20) was signed in a £40,000 transfer.

20: An early Christmas present as Latics received a £62,500 cash windfall following Tony Ellis's £250,000 move from Preston North End to Stoke City. Latics had sold Ellis to Preston for £23,000 two years earlier, but inserted a 25 per cent sell-on clause. Latics' Littlewoods Cup quarter-final, set for Wednesday, January 17th, was postponed due to the fourth-round replay involving Southampton and Swindon being called off because of a waterlogged pitch at The Dell. Due to a fixture pile-up, the nearest-available date was Tuesday, January 16th.

26: Earl Barrett marked his 100th Football League appearance with his first goal, the opener in a 2-1 Boxing Day home win against Port Vale.

30: Former soldier Guy Whittingham shot a first-half hat-trick as Portsmouth drew 3-3 at Boundary Park and threatened to inflict a first home loss on Latics for 26 matches. They led 2-0 after 10 minutes and 3-2 after an electrifying opening half. Mike Milligan saved the day for Latics with a late leveller.

JANUARY

1: Latics were denied a second win of the season at Leeds by a late equaliser from John Hendrie.

4: A transfer request, lodged by Andy Rhodes after the keeper was dropped for the New Year's Day match at Elland Road, was accepted by the club.

6: Frank Bunn's equaliser earned Latics a 1-1 draw at Third Division Birmingham City in the third round of the FA Cup as they almost became victims of a giantkilling act.

8: Manager Joe Royle admitted he was pursuing three transfer targets, but denied he had offered Neil Adams to Watford in exchange for Neil Redfearn. Latics would play Brighton in the fourth round of the FA Cup, providing they triumphed in their third-round replay.

'PINCH ME NOT'

10: In the absence of injured strike duo Frank Bunn and Andy Ritchie, winger Rick Holden was the match winner in a tense replay success over Birmingham.

11: The worst-kept secret came to fruition as Neil Redfearn completed a £150,000 move from Watford.

13: Injury-hit Latics lost 3-2 at Swindon, who vaulted over the Boundary Park side into third place.

15: Latics announced plans to join the jet set and hire a plane to fly them to Southampton for the quarter-final of the Littlewoods Cup after Saints defeated Swindon in their delayed fourth-round replay. Seventy-one fans were offered the chance to travel with the team.

18: The draw for the semi-finals of the Littlewoods Cup proved a complicated affair with all four quarters yet to be resolved. The winners of the Southampton/Latics tie would play either Derby or West Ham, while, in the other semi, Nottingham Forest or Tottenham would take on Sunderland or Coventry.

20: Latics were held 1-1 by Newcastle at Boundary Park, their sixth home league draw in 14 games, as manager Joe Royle admitted his side had become victims of their own success and visiting teams were invariably employing five-man defences.

24: High drama at The Dell, where Latics snatched a draw against Southampton in their Littlewoods Cup quarter-final thanks to a 94th-minute equaliser from Andy Ritchie. There was barely time for the restart when the final whistle sounded.

25: There was a furore after it was disclosed 600 Latics fans were locked out of the previous night's cup-tie and claims were made that the match ought to have been all-ticket. One area originally allocated to Latics fans was switched to home supporters on the night in order to ease congestion. Latics supporters were crammed into two pens instead of three and such was the overcrowding that some terrified followers feared another Hillsborough-scale tragedy.

27: Attention switched to the FA Cup as Latics came from behind to defeat Second Division rivals Brighton 2-1, Scott McGarvey and Andy Ritchie netting.

DIARY OF THE SEASON

31: The ninth major cup tie of the season and the third in eight days as Latics defeated Southampton 2-0 at Boundary Park, Andy Ritchie and Mike Milligan scoring the all-important goals. Chaddy The Owl made his debut against Saints. The cuddly creature, who would go on to become a celebrity in the footballing world, was the creation of Lois Best, a theatrical costume maker.

FEBRUARY

1: Chief Supt John Halliwell was hailed a hero for taking a "calculated gamble" and allowing Latics fans to stand alongside Southampton supporters on the Rochdale Road End. He made the decision 30 minutes before kick-off with home sections full and an estimated 4,000 fans outside the ground. The clamour for tickets began for the semi-final of the Littlewoods Cup against West Ham and visit of Everton in the fifth round of the FA Cup.

3: Latics twice came from behind on a gluepot pitch to draw 2-2 with West Brom at The Hawthorns.

5: The Littlewoods Cup semi-final against West Ham was already a 19,383 sell-out. Latics were offered a potential third route to Wembley when it was booked by the Football League to stage the end-of-season promotion play-off finals for the first time.

10: Substitute Roger Palmer came off the bench and scored to help set up a 2-0 home win against Stoke City.

12: Nick Henry was named North-West regional winner of the Barclays League Young Eagle award for January. Young reserve striker Andy Gayle was told he would not be retained at the end of the season and joined Stockport County on trial.

14: Latics produced a devastating display to demolish Lou Macari's West Ham United 6-0 at Boundary Park in an unforgettable first leg of their Littlewoods Cup semi-final. Supporters were in dreamland as a £1million Wembley pay-day was all but secured.

'PINCH ME NOT'

17: Another big cup date as Latics wiped out a two-goal deficit to force a 2-2 draw at home to First Division Everton in the fifth round of the FA Cup.

19: The draw for the quarter-finals of the FA Cup gave Latics or Everton a home tie against First Division leaders Aston Villa.

21: Further cup drama as Latics drew 1-1 at Everton in their fifth-round replay. This time the Toffees battled from behind to force a second replay, which would be at Boundary Park after Latics vice-chairman David Brierley won the toss of a coin to host the match. The Football Association ruled the second replay against Everton must be played on the date set for the return leg of the Littlewoods Cup semi-final against West Ham.

24: Stand-in striker Ian Marshall scored twice as Latics defeated Ipswich 4-1 at Boundary Park to strengthen their push for promotion.

25: Nottingham Forest lay in wait as Latics' would-be opponents in the final of the Littlewoods Cup. Forest, who completed a 2-1 aggregate win over Coventry City, would be making their fifth final appearance in 13 seasons.

JOE'S ROYLE MOMENT
Pictured showing off his third Jereboem of champagne of the season is Latics manager Joe Royle. Joe received the award along with an Ansley china plate and a cheque to the value of £250 for being voted 'Barclays Manager of the Month' for February.

27: More chaos for Latics as the second replay of their FA Cup fifth-round tie against Everton was called off because of storm damage at Boundary Park. The new date, Saturday, March 10, was also the date set aside for the club's FA Cup quarter-final home meeting with Graham Taylor's Aston Villa.

MARCH

3: Substitute Neil Adams scored the best goal of his career to earn lack-lustre Latics a lucky 1-1 draw at Brighton.

5: Neil Adams had talks with manager Joe Royle after being axed for Saturday's starting-line up at the Goldstone Ground.

6: Manager Joe Royle revealed keeper Andy Rhodes would be one of the two substitutes for the second leg of their Littlewoods Cup semi-final at West Ham in the event of Jon Hallworth being injured. Latics' fixture pile-up was such that the last eight and a half weeks of the season would see them having to play 15 league matches and a further six cup clashes.

7: Latics suffered their first defeat in 12 matches as they lost 3-0 at West Ham in the second leg of their Littlewoods Cup semi-final, but they still claimed their place at Wembley.

10: The epic FA Cup tie against Everton was finally resolved after 330 minutes as Latics won 2-1 after extra-time in the second replay. Toffees old-boy Ian Marshall scored the decisive goal.

12: Latics discovered they would play Manchester United in the semi-finals of the FA Cup if they overcame Aston Villa in the last eight.

13: Latics abandoned plans for a big-screen showing of their match against Aston Villa. They had hoped to show the match at Oldham Rugby League's Watersheddings ground, but were unable to find suitable screens. The idea was hatched after hundreds of fans were unable to get tickets.

14: Aston Villa became the latest team to be put to the sword as Latics overpowered the First Division leaders 3-0 to reach their first FA Cup semi-final since 1913. Latics consulted retired Manchester United secretary Les Olive for help in devising a plan to fairly distribute 30,000 tickets to fans for their Wembley appearance. It was announced that should any Latics player score a hat-trick at

'PINCH ME NOT'

Wembley, all 11 players and the two substitutes would each receive a new car from club sponsors Lookers at a cost of £100,000 to the local garage.

15: Latics were allocated 18,700 tickets for their FA Cup semi-final against Manchester United, who received 27,000.

16: Denis Irwin and Mike Milligan were named in the Eire 'B' squad to play England 'B' in Cork on March 27.

17: After the heady cup displays, it was back to earth with a bang in the league as Latics lost 1-0 at lowly Barnsley.

19: Manager Joe Royle confirmed he had made inquiries for several players before Thursday's transfer deadline.

20: Latics smashed their transfer record by splashing out £225,000 for Bournemouth striker Paul Moulden, who watched from the stands as his new club defeated his former one 4-0 at Boundary Park. Teenage midfield player Norman Kelly joined Swedish Second Division side Stromstad on a four-month loan.

A MAJOR MARCH OUTLAY.....Latics broke their transfer record by splashing out £225,000 on Paul Moulden.

22: Midfield man Gary Williams rejected a transfer-deadline day loan move to Wigan Athletic, preferring to remain and be part of the treble-seeking campaign. Reserve-team striker Stephen Morgan joined Fourth Division Wrexham on a one-month loan.

24: Latics made hard work of beating Hull City 3-2, having at one stage held a three-goal advantage.

27: Club sponsors Bovis and Intercity Property Group

hired a private jet to bring Mike Milligan and Denis Irwin home from Cork, where they had been making their debuts for Ireland 'B' in a 4-1 win against England 'B'.

28: The dash home proved a fruitless one as Latics lost at home to promotion rivals Sheffield United, their first defeat at Boundary Park in 14 months as they failed to stretch their unbeaten home record to 39 matches.

31: Andy Rhodes was back in goal for the 1-0 defeat at Middlesbrough. He had lost his place for the New Year's Day game at Leeds, where Jon Hallworth returned after a lengthy injury lay-off.

APRIL

2: Denis Irwin, Earl Barrett and Andy Ritchie were all named by their peers in the PFA Second Division team of the season.

3: Andy Ritchie returned after a month out, but could not prevent a 3-0 defeat at Leicester – hardly the ideal preparation for the FA Cup semi-final against Manchester United. It was a third straight league loss, all without Latics scoring.

8: Earl Barrett, Ian Marshall and Roger Palmer scored as Latics drew 3-3 against Manchester United after extra-time in an epic encounter at Maine Road.

9: Latics appealed to the Football League for permission to extend their season as they faced playing 11 games in 25 days.

11: There were tears of disappointment as opposed to joy as Latics failed to make it a Wembley double, losing 2-1 after extra-time in an equally enthralling cup semi-final replay, again at Maine Road.

12: Latics were told they could play their final league match against Bradford City 48 hours after the official end of the campaign.

13: Thirty eight hours after leaving Maine Road dejected, Latics were back in action with a noon shoot-out against champions-elect Leeds United at

'PINCH ME NOT'

THE ROYLE REPORT

A warm welcome to West Ham for the second time this season, who come here in resurgent form, occupying a place in the division just outside the play off zone. The Hammers have gathered momentum since the take over of Billy Bonds, and nobody ever doubted that once their multi talented squad got their act together, they would be a force to be reckoned with. Today's game takes on an even greater importance due to our own faltering away form. It was always going to be hard for the players to pick themselves up after the cup disappointment at Maine Road, but pick themselves up they did against League leaders Leeds united on Friday 13th. It's no secret that whilst the majority of our League don't relish the thought of playing Leeds, we certainly do! and a handsome 3-1 victory was more than justice over the ninety minutes. And so on to Port Vale, and an even bigger test, as there was never going to the 'rarified' atmosphere of Good Friday, and certainly not the exhilaration of Maine Road. We never got going in terms of our Good Friday performance, and has happened so often on our travels this term, schoolboy errors in our box allied to wayward finishing in the Vale's box, added up to another away day defeat. I'm completely puzzled by our away results and the same results have cost us dearly already, as with just a fair away record, we would be vieing for a top two spot, instead of joining the mad scramble for the play-offs.

There was certainly no sign of our aversion to grass in either leg of the Maine Road saga. Four goals and numerous other near misses were glowing proof that our supporters chants that 'we can play on grass as well' were not misplaced. Playing on grass has not been a problem all season, winning has. Once again our sincere thanks to every supporter who represented the Latics at Maine Road in the fashion that we have become accustomed to. I have had a vast mail bag in praise of the team and their efforts during two epic semi-finals, and there is no doubt that the town of Oldham, and it's team, is more firmly on the soccer map than ever before.

We need your support more than ever today for a game that certainly won't be 6-0. I feel that we have a lot in common with the 'Hammers' who like ourselves believe in passing the ball, and yet must wonder at times whether entertaining football is necessarily the formula to get out of this, the most competitive Second Division ever, but we aint changing.

See you soon.

JOE

8

PROUD MAN.....Joe Royle reflects in his programme notes on part one of the Manchester United semi-final epic.

Boundary Park. And they posted a 3-1 win, Rick Holden scoring two of the goals.

16: Latics failed to make it an Easter victory double, losing 2-0 on Monday at Port Vale, whose goals came from Darren Beckford. The striker would later become a key figure in Latics' run to the FA Cup semi-finals in 1994.

18: Hopes of a play-off place were dealt another blow with a 2-0 defeat at Plymouth, where Sean McCarthy, who would also join Latics, scored twice. Queues formed overnight outside Boundary Park as tickets went on open sale for the Littlewoods Cup final. By the time the office opened, they stretched 100 yards.

21: West Ham lost for the third time in four matches against Latics as they went down 3-0, a vital victory which kept alive Latics' promotion hopes.

24: Five days before Wembley and another tale of woe on the road as Latics lost 2-1 at Portsmouth, the 12th defeat on their league travels. It was also costly as Andy Holden returned after a calf strain only to suffer a recurrence, an injury which would keep him out of the final. Earl Barrett. Nick Henry, Earl Barrett and Frank Bunn all picked up knocks while Ian Marshall was still out with a thigh strain – hardly ideal preparations for the big day.

29: Latics failed to complete the fairytale, losing 1-0 to Nottingham Forest on a never-to-be-forgotten first visit to Wembley.

30: What an incredible home homecoming as a crowd estimated at 10,000 gathered outside the Civic Centre, where Latics were honoured with a civic reception. Thousands more lined a two-mile route as Latics paraded through Oldham on an open-top bus.

MAY

1: The home straight as Latics had their final four league games to play in the space of seven days which would determine their promotion fate. Latics were eight points off a top-six spot, but had played two fewer matches than their rivals. They could not have begun on a better note, beating Oxford United 4-1 at home, Rick Holden scoring a hat-trick.

3: Promotion hopes all but ended when Latics were held at home by Wolves, who, cruelly for Joe Royle's side, pinched a 1-1 draw with a late goal from substitute Tim Steele. The equaliser stunned the home fans and an eerie silence descended over Boundary Park.

5: Latics won for only the fourth time on their league travels, triumphing 3-2 at Sunderland, though other results meant a play-off spot was finally out of reach.

7: The curtain came down on a memorable campaign with a 1-1 draw at Bradford. Latics had been unbeaten in their four league games after Wembley, missing out on the play-offs by only three points – a great effort bearing in mind their schedule.

8: Earl Barrett was rewarded for a superb season as he was named as an over-age player by England for the under-21 Toulon Tournament in France.

'PINCH ME NOT'

9: Latics, already looking ahead to next season, completed the free-transfer signing of 19-year-old Ian Thompstone from Manchester City.

11: Kenny Dalglish pipped Joe Royle to become Barclays Bank Manager of the Year. Royle had captured three monthly awards – two divisional prizes and one national.

16: Striker Scott McGarvey signed for Japanese club Mazda, who were managed by Manchester United legend Bill Foulkes, in a £20,000 deal.

31: Roger Palmer signed a two-year contract extension, but Andy Rhodes rejected the offer of a new 12-month deal.

JUNE

6: Denis Irwin, having rejected a new three-year contract, signed for Manchester United in a £625,000 transfer, with a further £75,000 to be paid after he had won three full caps for Eire.

20: Andy Rhodes opened talks with Scottish club Dunfermline, for whom he would later sign.

What happened next

The spirit of the 'pinch-me season' has occasionally and briefly resurfaced for Latics on a number of occasions in the subsequent 20 years. There have been other memorable moments in both the FA Cup and League Cup in its various sponsorship guises, the highlight being a return to Wembley four years after they stepped out in the final of the Littlewoods Cup in 1990. Once again, though, there was a painful ending as Latics were cruelly denied a place in the final of the FA Cup after Mark Hughes scored a dramatic equaliser for Manchester United in the dying seconds of extra-time. Latics lost the replay 4-1 at Maine Road and one month later it became a double whammy as they were relegated from the Premier League.

The cup run of 1994 rekindled memories from four years earlier as Latics battled through to the last four. They overcame Derby, Stoke, Barnsley and Bolton – all teams from one division below the Premier League – to set up a repeat of the 1990 FA Cup semi-final. And there was the same outcome as Latics held the mighty Reds in the initial meeting before losing the replay. This time, the semi-finals were staged at Wembley, though the replay was at Maine Road, which had also been the venue for both matches four years earlier. And just as United won their first piece of silverware under Alex Ferguson in 1990 after overcoming Latics, there was also a hugely significant event when rivalries were renewed. United went on to win the double of league and FA Cup for the first time in their long and illustrious history.

In 1997, when Latics returned to English football's third tier by being relegated for the second time in three years, they again had to enter the FA Cup in the first round. And they have played non-league clubs Chelmsford, Hednesford, Barrow, Burton, Thurrock, Chasetown, Kettering and Kings Lynn, thankfully managing to avoid becoming victims of the sort of giantkilling acts they often used to perform. But there have been close scrapes, with Barrow, Burton and Chasetown, who are from the lowest part of the football pyramid, all taking them to replays.

'PINCH ME NOT'

Latics' most lucrative run in the League Cup, then sponsored by Worthington, came under Iain Dowie's management in 2002, when they reached the fourth round. After kicking off with a first-round victory against Notts County, they claimed the scalps of Derby and West Ham, both away, in the next two rounds. David Eyres and Clyde Wijnhard, with a penalty in extra-time, gave them a 2-1 victory at Pride Park while Canadian Carlo Corazzin was the matchwinner at the Premier League Hammers. They finally came unstuck in the last 16 by losing 2-0 at Crystal Palace.

The romance of the FA Cup was never better illustrated that in 2004/05 when Latics experienced both ends of the spectrum. They headed to non-league Thurrock in the opening round, then, two rounds later, were paired with neighbours Manchester City, a team two divisions higher in the structure of the game. Once again Latics, then managed by Brian Talbot, relished being the underdog as City were beaten 1-0 through a Scott Vernon goal which many believed hastened the exit of Kevin Keegan as manager. Sadly, Latics were unable to repeat the giantkilling against another Premier League team later the same month as Bolton won 1-0 at Boundary Park through an early goal from Ricardo Vaz Te.

Possibly the greatest cup upset since the 1989/90 season came in January 2008, when Latics, with John Sheridan at the helm, won 1-0 at top Premier League side Everton in the third round. Victory came through a spectacular matchwinner from

CHEST THE JOB........Gary McDonald shows more than just his delight following the stunning goal which set up Oldham's famous 2008 victory at Everton - also one of the stop-off points during the 'pinch-me season.' Picture courtesy of Tom Pickles.

WHAT HAPPENED NEXT

Gary McDonald which was followed by an equally impressive goal celebration involving pulling his shirt over his head and raising his arms at the same time – a dramatic shot which made many of the national newspapers. They were unable to progress further than the fourth round, though, as they were beaten by neighbours Huddersfield Town. Ironically, the only goal of the game came from Luke Beckett, who had two loan spells at Boundary Park in the three previous years.

There have also been other mouth-watering ties in which the outcome has not been favourable. Latics were beaten at Manchester United in the fourth round of the League Cup in 1991/92 and in the same competition have lost to Arsenal (1994), Newcastle (1996), Blackburn Rovers (2001) and Tottenham (2004), the latter recording a resounding 6-0 victory at Boundary Park. In the FA Cup, Chelsea came to town in 1999, when Latics lost 2-0 as player-manager Gianluca Vialli scored both goals. Chelsea were not the force of today but they were emerging as a top team and included Gianfanco Zola, Roberto Di Matteo, Marcel Desailly, Graeme Le Saux and a young John Terry.

Apart from the cup exploits, the last two decades have seen enormous fluctuations in fortunes at Boundary Park. Twelve months after the 'pinch-me season,' Latics finally reclaimed their top-flight place. It was in 1923 that they had last been among the elite, after which they plunged as low as the Fourth Division re-election places in some dark periods in the club's history. They went up in style in 1991, however, claiming the Second Division title with virtually the last kick of the campaign when they came from 2-0 down after an hour to defeat Sheffield Wednesday 3-2.

BEWARE THE BULL.......Latics came up with something better than the two-goal blast the Wolves striker produced at Molineux in August, 1990. Ian Marshall hit a hat-trick to secure a 3-2 away victory on the opening day of the club's promotion-winning season.

'PINCH ME NOT'

That triumph was followed by three memorable years dining at football's top table as the First Division became the Premier League. Latics were founder members and experienced some dramatic moments, such as the 'Great Escape' of 1993 when they won their last three matches – at title-chasing Aston Villa and at home to Liverpool and Southampton to stay up on goal difference at the expense of Crystal Palace. The fairytale came to an end with relegation from the Premier League in 1994, since when there has been a steady decline.

Two demotions in three years saw them languish in what is now Coca-Cola League One, where they have been since 1997. Indeed, they are the longest-serving team in that division. Latics have also had to endure a number of crises and the mood didn't come any darker than when the club entered administration in 2003 after owner Chris Moore withdrew his funding. Luckily, the 'Three Amigos' – New York-based businessmen Simon Blitz, Simon Corney and Danny Gazal – came to the rescue with a takeover which has provided stability.

Quite what the next 20 years holds in store remains to be seen as Latics are still striving to relocate to a new stadium in Failsworth to replace the antiquated Boundary Park, which has been their home since 1906. The owners believe the only way the club can survive in the long term is by moving to a new, purpose-built stadium which can offer the new revenue streams needed to subsidise the playing side.

Celebrities savour success

Latics hit the right note

Musician Graham Lambert was certainly in tune with Latics' exploits of the 1989/90 season. They were halcyon days for both the club and the Inspiral Carpets, the indie rock band of which Lambert was a founder member and guitarist. He began watching Latics play in the third tier of English football in the 1970s and recalled of the 'pinch-me' era : "It was an exciting time, not only for Latics but also the band, which was taking off at that time. We had been plying our trade playing back rooms of pubs in Oldham for the previous three or four years hoping for a break, but suddenly things took off. We had our first top 20 hit 'This Is How It Feels' and went on tour to promote our first album 'Life', which made it to no 2 in the charts."

Inspiral Carpets were on tour at the time of the final of the Littlewoods Cup, but luckily had no gig on the Sunday night. They had played Sheffield's Octagon Theatre on the Saturday and all five band members – Lambert was the only Latics fan – plus a couple of roadies and two employees from their record company set off for Wembley in a people carrier the following morning.

Though Latics lost to Nottingham Forest, Lambert says it was a great day as he proudly watched his team walk out on the hallowed turf. And one of his most abiding memories is the night following the final when Inspiral Carpets resumed their tour in Nottingham, of all places. He said: "We were playing Rock City and, when we walked on stage to 2,000 fans, there were chants of 'Brian Clough's red and white army.' It was well known we were an Oldham band and that night is one which has always stuck in my mind."

Lambert, who still lives in Chadderton, also recalls the band doing a photo session with the Latics players on the artificial pitch at Boundary Park for the football

'PINCH ME NOT'

WHERE MUSIC MEETS FOOTBALL........Frank Bunn, Andy Ritchie and Nick Henry get up close and personal with Graham Lambert and the other members of the Inspiral Carpets indie band. The acquaintance was made for a feature for the popular Shoot football magazine.

magazine 'Shoot' in the build-up to the final. "There was Frank Bunn, Andy Ritchie, Andy Rhodes and Nick Henry and it again showed how the wider world had taken note not only of Latics but also the band," he explained. Another memory is getting the night train to and from London, where he had been working on the album, on several occasions, so he did not miss the big cup matches.

He continued: "I remember doing that for the Littlewoods Cup quarter-final replay against Southampton and also the FA Cup quarter-final against Aston Villa. I was determined not to miss those games." The occasions were more special for him because he says there were a number of 'grim' seasons in Joe Royle's early years at Boundary Park. But, from 1986/87, when Latics reached the Second Division play-offs, he could detect better times were ahead. "Joe had begun to assemble a good team and I thought as long as we could keep it together – unlike previous years when we had to sell our best players – we had a chance," he added. "We had Andy Ritchie, who was our Wayne Rooney, while Frank Bunn was an unsung hero. Many only remember Bunn for the six goals he scored against Scarborough, but the way he led the attacking line was wonderful and he also did a lot of unselfish work for others.

"We also had Earl Barrett and Paul Warhurst, who had electrifying pace at the back, Mike Milligan and Nick Henry in the middle and Roger Palmer still scoring goals. Rick Holden was signed just before the start of the season and was the final piece of the jigsaw. The team ticked all the boxes and I could see the potential of the side and it therefore came as no surprise when we beat the likes of Arsenal, Aston Villa and Southampton – something which was unheard of for a small club like ourselves. We did so by playing brilliant football and we were not only rubbing shoulders with these big clubs, but were their equals and were certainly not in awe of them."

Lambert admits the plastic pitch was obviously a help, but pointed out the side also produced some excellent performances on grass. He said: "We drew at First Division sides Southampton and Everton and who will ever forget the 3-3 draw against Manchester United in the FA Cup semi-final at Maine Road? It wasn't just about the Astroturf, though that surface encouraged you to play good football, which we did."

Latics remain close to Lambert's heart – as was seen on a tour a couple of years ago, when he incorporated some shots from the glory days into a slide show which formed a backdrop to their set.

Jack's fairytale storyline

Jack Crawshaw, who had a distinguished career in television, never believed he would witness a storyline which had Latics playing at Wembley. If he were ever to compile his own personal 'This Is Your Life', the programme he produced for many years, it would contain a footballing theme centred on his beloved Latics because he was six when first taken to a match at Boundary Park in the late 1940s by his father, also named Jack. And, from over 60 years following the club's fortunes, he says the 1989/90 season remains the one he will never forget.

Crawshaw, who also followed Manchester United in the era of the Busby Babes, recalled: "I went to the 1957 FA Cup final, when United lost to Aston Villa, and remember leaving Wembley feeling drained. I wondered how I would cope if Latics ever reached Wembley, never for one moment believing they ever would." But that

'PINCH ME NOT'

dream become a reality 33 years later for a fan born at Royal Oldham Hospital, which overlooks Boundary Park.

The 1989/90 season produced some amazing memories, none more so than the Littlewoods Cup win against reigning First Division champions Arsenal, and Crawshaw, who still does freelance writing and media consultancy work, said: "I was working in London and would see most of the games when Latics came to play in the capital. I also went to Boundary Park whenever I could for games and one of them was the Arsenal cup tie. I was never so proud of Latics as I was that night. I have been watching them for over 60 years and that was the best I had ever seen them play. I never had any doubt they would win."

Crawshaw has some great memories of the 'pinch-me season', with the Wembley final the crowning glory. He says it was a great family day out with the party including his father, great-aunt Doris, nephew Adam, wife-to-be Lynne and friend John Riley. His cousin is Rod Adams, a Latics director at the time. And when the family were walking down Wembley Way, he says they spotted Adams on the stadium balcony surveying the crowds.

Latics took 30,000 fans to the final and Crawshaw remembers it as one of the greatest days the town has ever had. "It was like Oldham Wakes because the whole town went to the same place at the same time. You were 200 miles away, yet it was like home as you were surrounded by people you knew. I remember bumping into Harry Travis, a teacher from my days at Chadderton

SUITABLY ATTIRED ....Jack Crawshaw happy and proud in the colours of his beloved Latics.

Grammar School, on Wembley Way. We used to call him 'FA Cup' at school because of his large ears and here he was framed between the Twin Towers, which was a surreal moment. Great aunt Doris, who could well have been in her eighties, was dressed for the occasion. She was wearing an overcoat and never removed it, even though it was a scorching hot day. Those are the sort of things from the day which remain etched in my memory 20 years later."

He explained that two of the pinnacles of his television career were directing the FA Cup final replay between Manchester United and Brighton in 1983, along with the same job at an England v Denmark international. "They were special moments, but nothing compared to the feeling when Joe Royle led out the Latics team on to the famous Wembley turf in 1990," he continued. "There was never any question of divided loyalties with me having watched United as well. The two clubs could not have been further apart as United were in the First Division and Latics in Third Division North. I knew that dual loyalty would never be put to the test as the two teams had never previously met and there was little likelihood of them doing so."

But the two teams did so in 1974 after Latics had been promoted and United relegated. Crawshaw was at Boundary Park to see the Jimmy Frizzell's side record a famous 1-0 victory against the Reds. And, when it came to the crunch, it was Latics, his home-town team, who Crawshaw rooted for. The same applied in 1990, when he was shouting for Latics in their two epic FA Cup semi-finals against the Old Trafford side.

Crawshaw says Andy Ritchie was the player he particularly admired, describing him as an inspirational figure who was, and still is, adored by the fans. "When Andy was on the park, there was always the chance something exciting would happen and we would win the game. I was also fond of Rick Holden, who was unique on the left with his extraordinary shaped left foot, which enable him to cross the ball with great accuracy for the likes of Ritchie, Bunn and Palmer."

Alex too young to remember

Hollyoaks and Emmerdale actor Alex Carter's one regret about Latics' 'pinch-me season' is that he was not old enough to appreciate what it meant. "I was only seven and assumed it was normal for Latics to reach a cup final," he explained. It was only later that the enormity of what they achieved became clear – and that it might be a once-in-a-lifetime occurrence.

Carter, who as a schoolboy used to operate the electronic scoreboard at Boundary Park on matchdays with his friend Nick Hardy, is sad that he cannot remember more about Wembley and the rest of that never-to-be-forgotten campaign. He said: "I have since watched the final on video, but, as for the day, I am afraid it is something of a blur. I can remember things about the journey, but not about the match itself. We stayed with an aunt and uncle in Balham and we used one of their bed sheets as a flag. We wrote 'Delph Latics' on the bed sheet and I can also recall little things like the marker pen damaging the kitchen table."

PUT IN THE PICTURE......that's Alex Carter, who had to be told, gently, that Wembley trips weren't commonplace for Latics.

He also recalls an amusing anecdote from the build-up to the final, when he and his mother Edith met Latics' left back in Smiths Do-It-All. Andy Barlow had been pictured in the newspapers eating a local delicacy – pudding on a muffin. "I asked Andy for his autograph and even my mum knew who he was as she was asking him about pudding on a muffin, which is gorgeous." Carter is from a family of diehard Wolves fans, but came to live in Oldham when his father relocated through work when he was three months old. "My dad decided to support the local team, though he remains a Wolves fan," he added. "As for me, Latics have always been my team."

Right lyrics for Laurie

Latics' successes in 1989/90 were music to the ears of Laurie Holloway, who can remember when the club languished in football's basement division. The composer and musical director has seen more lean times than he can recall since first watching his beloved Latics in the late 1940s. So, to see them knocking out First Division teams

CELEBRITIES SAVOUR SUCCESS

like Arsenal and Southampton en route to the Littlewoods Cup final was something he could scarcely believe. "When I used to watch Latics in Third Division North in the days of George Hardwick, Eric Gemmell and Ray Haddington, I never imagined that one day they would reach the final of a major cup competition," he said.

Holloway, who was born within walking distance of Boundary Park, may live in exile near Maidenhead, but his love for Latics has never diminished. Whenever they are playing in London, the former musical director to Michael Parkinson's chat show endeavours to get to watch them – as he has done for many years. Sadly, during the 'pinch-me season', he was only occasionally able to see the team because of work commitments, though he says he was always with the team in spirit.

That love stemmed from Latics being ingrained into his heart as a youngster, his mother Annie having been a season-ticket holder who he would go with as well as two aunts. They would also travel to away matches. He later stood on the terracing at the Chaddy End, often cycled to away games and can recall one trip to Doncaster with neighbour Peter Haslam as they went over the tops via Holmfirth in heavy rain.

While Holloway missed the Littlewoods Cup final, he did make it to Wembley four years later with his late wife Marion Montgomery to see Latics play Manchester United in the semi-finals of the FA Cup, when they were cruelly denied a place in the final by a last-gasp Mark Hughes equaliser.

Holloway has worked with many of the world's top artistes, including Judy Garland, Liza Minnelli, Sammy Davis jnr, Elaine Paige, Englebert Humperdinck, Dames Cleo Lane and Kiri te Kanawa, as well as composing theme tunes for programmes such as Blind Date, Game for a Laugh and Beadle's About.

WORK PALS, FOOTBALL FOES........Barnsley supporter Michael Parkinson and Oldham fanatic Laurie Holloway.

The fans' say

Janet Chadwick received a telephone call at her home in Australia from Cilla Black, who informed her that the television programme 'Surprise, Surprise' had arranged a trip for her to Wembley. Twenty years on, she retells her story:

I followed the events of the 'pinch-me season' from afar in absolute disbelief and I often wondered why the team had waited until I had left the country to perform miracles on the pitch. It was typical of my luck that I had missed the most amazing season in the club's history after hardly ever being away from Boundary Park until emigrating to Australia in 1987. I felt cheated, as though they had somehow done it on purpose just to spite me. After all, my friends and I had often joked that we would have to wait until we were in our wheelchairs to see them play at Wembley.

My family, who were all diehard Latics fans, knew exactly how I was feeling and took great pleasure in telephoning me after every incredible result. I still remember Jill, my hysterical sister, screaming down the line after we had defeated West Ham 6-0. I couldn't bear the thought of every single member of my family going to Wembley without me. So, after assessing my finances, I tried to book a flight to Manchester, but could not find one and had begun to panic. I was getting ready to leave for work when the telephone rang again and, expecting it to be my sister wanting to know whether I had finally booked a flight, I allowed my three-year-old daughter to answer. I heard her tell the person on the other end of the line that I was on the toilet and she would get me. When I eventually answered it was not my sister, but Cilla Black, who was recording the television show 'Surprise, Surprise.'

I have no idea what I said to her as I was stunned as well as embarrassed about the whole of England knowing I was sitting on the loo when she called. Cilla explained that Jill was determined I would not miss out on Wembley so she had written to the programme to ask if they could sort flights for me. She was ringing to

THE FANS' SAY

THE PROUDEST MOMENT......and well worth flying across the world for. The Latics fans hail their heroes during the well-deserved lap of honour.

say she had done that and also arranged for me to meet the players. Soon, my daughter and I were on our way back to England and I started chatting to somebody sitting across the aisle on the plane and he told me he was going to watch his team play in the final of the Littlewoods Cup. I enquired whether he was a Nottingham Forest fan, but he replied 'Latics' and said he had been waiting all his life for this moment. I wondered as we chatted how many more of us were making the same pilgrimage. I knew of at least one more – my father, who travelled from Canada for this famous day in history.

The big day arrived and I climbed on to the coach with my family and friends, who I had earlier joked with about us needing wheelchairs for this special day. Happily, we didn't need them. The atmosphere at Wembley was awesome and I had never been so proud to be a Latics fan. It brought a tear to my eye to glimpse the sea of blue and white in the stadium for the first time. The whole day, except the result, was special. And though it didn't go our way, I still had one of the best days of my life. Flying back to Australia, I thought how I owed it all to my sister, who made it possible with a letter to Cilla Black. It also made me realise how much I had missed throughout the rest of the season and I felt even more cheated!

'PINCH ME NOT'

Carl Marsden was a pupil at Hulme Grammar during the 'pinch-me season' and he recalls one particular story from his schooldays.

My English teacher at Hulme, an Everton fan, was somebody I couldn't stand the sight of. When he found out, however, that touts at school were trying to charge me £30 for a ticket for the Littlewoods Cup semi-final against West Ham, he acted. I was from a comparatively poor family and was on an assisted place. He pulled me to one side the day before the match and I thought he was going to give me detention for something like late work. Imagine my shock when he handed me a free ticket to the Chaddy End for the game – one he had confiscated from the touts.

He had taken the touts to task and instigated his own sense of justice and fair play. Funnily enough, he became my favourite teacher after that and thereafter I soared from near bottom to top of the class. I was given a random lift to that game by a car load of West Ham fans and they were full of banter. I even had a pint with them before the game. They arranged to meet me in the car park afterwards, but I later found out they had left well before the end. I looked for them in London on the return, one of several days I rang in sick, but again had no joy.

Michael Clarke was another schoolboy who still has vivid memories of that never-to-be-forgotten season. He writes:

I was only nine or ten at the time and remember going to the toilet in the Littlewoods Cup tie against Arsenal and missing Andy Ritchie's first goal. I heard the roar of the crowd and thought Arsenal must have scored, but thinking it was remarkably loud for the away side. Latics could not possibly be 1-0 ahead against the league champions, could they? My dad recalls the 2-2 draw at Southampton. He telephoned me to ask what the final score was. When I told him it was 2-2, he said I must be wrong because it had been 1-0 to Southampton with 10 minutes left. Again, that was the beauty of the season. Latics seemed to do the impossible every time they took to the field in those games against the top teams.

The Everton match at Boundary Park was a highlight. I remember watching the highlights on Match of the Day over and over again. How did a Division Two side come back from 2-0 down against Everton? It defied belief. I also remember the Ian Marshall goal in the replay. I seem to recall the commentator saying that Rick Holden swung his boot like a 'sand iron' to cross for Marshy's header. I remember my dad and me meeting Ian Marshall at the Grey Mare in Royton a few weeks after the second replay against Everton, in which he had scored with a penalty. I was completely star-struck to meet him, but I recall my dad discussing with him penalty techniques.

I can also remember queuing for Aston Villa tickets, and they were crazy Boundary Park standards. Everyone was very friendly and upbeat joking with each other and talking about their expectations. A good cup has that sort of effect on a town.

As for the match, we crushed them. They didn't stand a chance by that stage of the cup run, nor did poor old West Ham! The season had a flat finish – think how many matches we played – but it inspired my dad and me to get season tickets and a love of the club that will never die.

Steve Laithwaite recalls the panic of losing eight Wembley match tickets for himself and his mates and the unexpected happy ending.

Back in 1990, I was a 19-year-old lad working in Rochdale and there were eight of us who were heading for Wembley – or so we all thought. For some reason, I ended up looking after all eight tickets and kept them safe in my wallet until one fateful day. During my lunch hour a couple of weeks before the final, I went into Rochdale town centre to get money from the cash machine. Later that day, I was asked by a colleague to show them the tickets....disaster! I was unable to produce the wallet containing the match and train tickets, along with my £40 and cash cards. I searched everywhere and my boss had about 20 members of staff helping before I reported the loss to Rochdale Police and also called the Yorkshire Bank, where I'd withdrawn the money. Nothing had been handed in.

As all the tickets for the match had been sold, I was totally heartbroken about the possibility of not getting to the game. I also wondered how I was going to tell everyone and how I was also going to pay everyone. I earned £105 per week, but the match tickets were £28 each and there was the train fare as well to pay back. We all played pool

ENTER VIA
BANQUETING HALL

WEMBLEY
STADIUM LIMITED

Littlewoods

CHALLENGE CUP

PRESS
BOX

Sunday, 29th April 1990
Kick Off 3.00 p.m.
You are advised to take up your
position by 2.15 p.m.

SEAT
Nº   078

TO BE RETAINED

'PINCH ME NOT'

together two nights a week and saw each other every night and I managed to avoid the subject all week while I worked out how to tell everyone while holding on to the faint hope of finding the wallet. On the Monday of Wembley week, when everyone was full of high spirits about the game. I went to work knowing I had to tell them soon.

I called the police and bank one last time, but had no luck and spent the rest of the morning working out my speech about the lost tickets and how sorry I was. My boss then shouted me into his office to say I had a call which was nothing unusual at this point. I was asked to confirm my name, colour of the lost wallet, its contents and where I had lost it. I was then told it was the Yorkshire Bank and someone had just handed it in. If I brought identification, I could collect it. I was driven into Rochdale by my boss, who told me to remain calm as everything might not be in the wallet. But when I found the only thing not in there was the cash, I celebrated like I had done at the final whistle following the 6-0 semi-final win against West Ham. Apart from my work colleagues, I never told anyone about the lost tickets until we were back in the Abbeylee pub on the Sunday night after returning from Wembley. It was a fantastic and proud day watching the boys in blue at Wembley in a cup final....but it nearly didn't happen.

Graham Anderson's tears following Latics' Littlewoods Cup defeat were shared by the nation.

At the end of the game at Wembley, I, like many of the other Latics fans, was extremely disappointed and in tears. Unbeknown to me, the television cameras were trained on me and pundits in the studio were talking about me. It was only when I returned home and was walking through Oldham town centre on the Monday morning that people kept coming over me to shake hands and commiserate. They all mentioned they had seen me on television, but I hadn't a clue what had happened.

I was not able to forget the moment as it was repeated regularly on the 'Saint and Greavsie' football preview show every time Oldham was mentioned. I think the clip was shown about 28 times. It was a glorious weekend and a group of 20 us went from the Bridge Inn on Moorhey Street and stayed at the Dominion Hotel in the West End of London. On the Saturday, we went to watch Brentford v Blackpool and initially the police did not know which end to put us in as there were about 150 of us. In the end, we were put in with the Blackpool fans and the Brentford supporters began singing 'come on Oldham' and that was a good day.

THE FANS' SAY

CRYING SHAME......oh so close for Latics as a falling Neil Adams goes within a whisker of finding the well-guarded Forest net at Wembley.

On the morning of the final, the 20 of us went to a working men's club not far from Wembley and Paul Smith was worse for wear from the night before. He fell asleep and we had a few pranksters among us. We cleared all the glasses away, had a word with the steward and turned forward his watch and the clock in the club. We went into another room and got the steward to go and wake him. Paul asked what time it was and the steward replied: "Look at your watch." It showed quarter past four. When he saw that, he sobered up instantly as he thought he had missed the match when, in fact, it was only one o'clock.

There was another incident from the Littlewoods Cup quarter-final at Southampton which I can remember. I was lucky to get into the ground, but there were between 600 and 700 who were locked out as the match was not all-ticket. In those days, matches weren't televised live as they are today, so the unfortunate fans went into a local pub, where the landlord extracted the Michael out of them. When they enquired about the score, he told them Southampton were winning 1-0, 2-0, 2-1, 3-1 and so on. They carried on drinking and were totally fed up. When news came through we had not lost, they extracted revenge on the pub. The cigarette machine from the pub ended up on the special train Latics had chartered to take fans to the game. It was supposed to be 'dry', but on the way back it sounded like a steam train as all the cans were opened.

They were heady days and a far cry to the hard times. I have been supporting Latics for over 40 years and remember going to Workington for a midweek match when there were 12 of us, but here we were taking 30,000 fans to Wembley.

Tony Hardman tells how the Gods conspired for him to miss the semi-finals of both the Littlewoods Cup and FA Cup.

My most abiding memory of the 'pinch-me season' was fate conspiring against me to ensure I didn't see any of the semi-final ties that ordinarily I would have been at. I had a ticket for the match against West Ham at Boundary Park, only to wake up on the morning of the game with a sore throat so bad that it felt as though I was swallowing barbed wire. The doctor diagnosed tonsillitis and prescribed me a cocktail

EARL EXCITES......even defender Earl Barrett got in on the scoring act in the 6-0 Littlewoods Cup semi-final slaughter of West Ham, driving home from close range.

THIS ONE'S FOR ABSENT FRIENDS.......a Stitch-in-time moment for Andy Ritchie as the striker celebrates his equaliser in the FA Cup semi-final replay against Manchester United – much to the despair of Gary Pallister.

of drugs, which I eagerly started to take in the hope that, by 6.30pm, I would have made a full recovery. I blatantly lied to my parents – telling them I was fine and would wrap up extra warm. But Dad ignored my protestations and I was left to listen to the game on the radio, though I did negotiate a later bedtime, so I could watch the highlights on television.

Missing the FA Cup semi-finals was the result of a school ski trip. It had been booked in September for the following April, with me thinking football would not interfere with my plans as we would be mid-table by then and out of both cups. Of course Latics reached the semi-final and, instead of being at Maine Road, I found myself on a French glacier trying to find BBC World Service to listen to the match. We ended up getting the scores relayed to us by telephoning home. But such was the level of mistrust between Latics and United fans that everyone queued to use the payphone to check the final scores.

Michael Dunkerley reveals how he was amusingly mistaken for a politician of a blue persuasion when he arrived at his brother's home en route to Wembley.

'PINCH ME NOT'

My younger brother Colin, who had moved to St Albans in 1989, was delighted when I was able to obtain a final ticket for us both. I stayed at his house for the weekend and thought I would greet him on my arrival by wearing by bob hat, scarf and rosette, all of which were blue and white. At the precise moment I opened my car door in the driveway, a man, who was wearing a blue and white rosette, but no scarf or bob hat, walked past me towards the front door. He spoke about me wearing so much blue and how pleased he was to see me and asked what my involvement was in Conservative politics. Our initial conversation was somewhat confusing until the person introduced himself not as a Latics supporter, but Peter Lilley, MP for St Albans and Financial Secretary to the Treasury in Mrs Thatcher's Government. He was on his rounds, delivering leaflets prior to the forthcoming election. My recollection is of a jovial conversation about jumping to conclusions. He wished the team well but, sadly, it was not to be.

Margaret McGrath relates her fond memories of a family day out at Wembley when her late husband Terry became a celebrity supporter.

We went to Wembley as a family – me, Terry and our two young boys, Ryan and Liam – and hired our own coach with friends. In those days, Frank Sidebottom was the rage and a friend made Terry, who used to be a steward on the car park at Boundary Park, a similar outfit with oversized blue shorts, which were down to his ankles, and a big, blue and white flat cap. When we arrived at Wembley, Terry disappeared to the toilet and we wondered where he had got to as he was away for so long. He eventually returned, saying somebody asked to take his photograph and, by the time they had finished, a queue had formed with others wanting to do the same.

We went as a family to see the team at the civic reception and, when they were on the balcony, the fans were singing 'come on Elsie' as Elsie Shaw was the Mayor at the time. Sadly, Terry died of cancer ten years ago, but I still look back at the happy day we had as a family at Wembley.

Ian Cheeseman will never forget April 29th 1990 as, hours after his first child Steven was born, he dashed to Wembley to commentate on the final of the Littlewoods Cup for the Royal Oldham Hospital's Radio Cavell.

In the days before I began my broadcasting career on BBC Radio Manchester, I worked at the Co-operative Bank in Manchester and had a Sunday morning show on

THE FANS' SAY

Radio Cavell. It was a general music programme, in which I played requests and sometimes interviewed politicians, actors etc. When Latics reached the final of the Littlewoods Cup, I was asked to be part of the commentary team and was excited at the prospect of covering a match at Wembley. My wife Irene was pregnant and the baby was due on April 22nd, so I thought the birth would be well before the game.

I became increasingly anxious, though, as the countdown to Wembley continued and there was no sign of the baby. Then, late on the eve of the final, there were the first labour pains and Irene was admitted to the Royal Oldham Hospital in the early hours of Sunday morning. The midwife thought it would be a long labour, so I thought there would be no chance of me getting to Wembley. The window at the end of the maternity ward overlooked the Sheepfoot Lane and at seven o'clock I could hear lots of noise outside as a fleet of coaches left the ground for Wembley before it became peaceful once more. Things suddenly gathered pace and Steven was born shortly after nine o'clock and Wembley was the last thing on my mind as I sat like any proud father holding his new-born baby.

It was Irene who suggested I should go to Wembley. She knew how I had been looking forward to it. She added it might be the only chance I would have to commentate at Wembley and I ought to go if I could still make it to the game. I left at 10.30am and drove. By going so late, I had no problems on the roads and I arrived shortly after two o'clock. Kent Wells and I shared the commentary and Irene sat in the hospital listening. I even had a spare programme, which I asked Andy Ritchie to sign to the little boy who was born on the day Latics played at Wembley. It was a unique day I shall never forget.

MAGICAL MOMENT......Joe Royle proudly leads his side out at Wembley and engages frequent visitor Brian Clough in friendly conversation.

189

'PINCH ME NOT'

Joan Faulkner remembers a trip to Latics' shop during the 'pinch-me season.'

It was almost Christmas 1989 and I had gone to the Latics shop to buy presents for my two sons when Andy Ritchie came in. He was choosing a new pair of football boots and sat down to try them on, not far from where I was standing. There was an elderly lady in the shop, who was obviously not familiar with our players as she went over to Andy and asked: "Excuse me, do you work here?" He replied: "Well, I suppose you could say that." She went on to ask him for help, so he referred her to one of the shop assistants. If only she had known she'd been talking to one of our greatest-ever players. It still amuses me.

Chris England, a London-based Latics fan, recalls some of his vivid memories after making umpteen motorway journeys to see all the big games.

I was at Blackburn for the first game of the season when Rick Holden made his debut and remember thinking he didn't look like a footballer. Then, in the FA Cup semi-final replay against Manchester United, he tormented right-back Mike Phelan. The ball went into touch and Rick went to take a quick throw, but there was nobody near him, so he threw the ball against Phelan's back, collected it and ran past him. I thought: Now that IS a footballer! In that game, Andy Ritchie scored our equaliser and I jumped up too quickly, blacked out and woke up sitting down again.

I drove from London for the first game against United. En route, I tuned in to follow Palace's dramatic 4-3 victory over Liverpool in the other semi and caught sight from the M6 of a brightly sunlit Villa Park, where it was being played. I recall thinking it was one of the best days football had given me. And that was before our game – the best

HE LOOKS LIKE A FOOTBALLER NOW........Rick Holden (right) celebrates at Upton Park with Neil Adams.

WELL WORTH ALL THE MOTORWAY MILES FOR FAR-FLUNG FANS.....Andy Ritchie and Steve Bruce sum up the tension of FA Cup semi-final day.

I had ever seen. We were behind the goal and everybody was standing on seats. It looked and felt like a terrace, except that we were quite precariously balanced.

When we were leading Aston Villa 3-0 in the FA Cup quarter-final, we already knew we were playing United next and the fans were singing "Bye in the semi, we've got a bye in the semi." For some games, I had to take a day off work, drive from London to queue at the ticket office, then drive home – a nine-hour round trip. I listened to Nelson Mandela's release on the radio on one of those ticket runs. We had little blue plastic membership cards, which staff punched a hole in for the big games. After the first FA Cup semi at Maine Road, I drove to Stockport to give the card to a friend, who then used it on the Monday to buy me a ticket for the replay.

We had lost the unstoppable momentum by the time the Littlewoods Cup final came round. I was disappointed, of course, but the tension slipped away at full-time and I started to enjoy the day. It was the best season I'd ever experienced, then it was straight into Italia 90. I can also remember every kick of that. There was even a newspaper article seriously suggesting Andy Ritchie should be included in Bobby Robson's England squad for the World Cup alongside Lineker, Beardsley and Bull.

'PINCH ME NOT'

Alan Miller recalls the desperate measures some of his work-mates resorted to as they were determined not to miss the Littlewoods Cup quarter-final at Southampton.

I was working on a building site at Derker and was telling some of the lads when were having our morning brew that I was going to the match. They were apprentices who wouldn't have been more than 17 or 18 and had no money. At lunchtime, all the workers used to give these lads their money to go to the chippy in the works van. They filled it up with petrol on the firm's account and drove to Southampton, where they used the dinner money to buy tickets for the game. Needless to say, when they reported for work the next morning, they were sacked.

Andy Halliwell relates a deeply moving personal story from one of the greatest nights of the 'pinch-me season.'

The thought of league champions Arsenal visiting Boundary Park in the fourth round of the Littlewoods Cup was something to behold for a Latics fan aged 12. I had never been to a match of this scale in the three years I had been following the team. Sadly, on the morning of the match, my grandmother died. Knowing how much I'd been looking forward to going to the game, my mother, despite being beside herself with grief, took the noble decision not to tell me the news when I returned home from school. Both she and my father kept up the facade all evening as we went to the match and I was only given the sad news the following morning. Needless to say, I was upset because this was my first experience of death.

I also remember the mental torture of listening to the quarter-final at Southampton on the wireless in my bedroom – in 1990, a 12-year-old boy's technology was still primitive. We were 2-1 down in stoppage time and referee Roger Milford was looking at his watch. I looked skyward with tears in my eyes and thought: 'Please Gran, help us!' Cue the commentary and Andy Ritchie's last-gasp goal. Pandemonium! I knew we would beat them in the replay on the plastic. The memories are still vivid. I can shut my eyes and still see the royal blue carpet in my bedroom.

Not many years ago, I was invited to the Football Writers' dinner in London, where I now work in advertising, and plucked up courage to introduce myself to Joe Royle. I regaled him with the story about the Arsenal match and he listened intently as we discussed just how magical the years between 1989 and 1994 had been for all of us.

Where are they now?

Neil Adams: He is employed to give his views on Norwich City as a pundit for BBC Radio Norfolk and is also a columnist on the Norwich Evening News as well as being assistant coach of the under-18 team at Carrow Road.

Andy Barlow: Since retiring, he has spent the last 10 years working as a regional coach for the Professional Footballers' Association. He has been at Boundary Park regularly this season, helping a group of Latics players achieve their coaching badges.

Earl Barrett: Coaches the under-16s at Stoke City and works with their under-13s and 14s, all part-time. He also coaches the under-16s and 19s at Salford City College. Since retiring, he has worked at Latics' centre of excellence, Manchester City's Academy and as a sports co-ordinator for City's Football In The Community programme. As an extra, he works for the Press Association at various matches.

Chris Blundell: Lives in Stockport, where he has had his own security business for the last eight years. He is still involved in football, coaching Cheadle and Gatley under-10s.

Frank Bunn: Is currently first-team coach at Coca-Cola Championship club Coventry City. Since a knee injury forced his early retirement, he has also coached the youngsters at Wigan Athletic and Manchester City. Iain Dowie took him to the Ricoh Arena in 2007.

Willie Donachie: Was recently appointed assistant Academy director at Newcastle United after returning home from the Caribbean following a two-year stint as the national coach in Antigua.

'PINCH ME NOT'

Jon Hallworth: The goalkeeper made Oldham his home after retiring and is currently living in Springhead. In his new life outside football, he works in property development.

Nick Henry: Since finishing his playing career at non-league Scarborough, whom he managed, he has stayed in the seaside resort. His partner Tracey is the licensee of the The Albert and Henry pub, and he assists with the running.

MIDDLE MAN........Nick Henry in action at Wembley in the memorable spring of 1990 and now resident on the North Yorkshire coast.

Wayne Heseltine: Still lives in his home-city Bradford, where the former Manchester United and Latics left-back has had his own flooring business for the last 12 years.

Andy Holden: After leaving the coaching staff at Boundary Park in 1997 following Neil Warnock's arrival, he has spent the last 13 years at Everton, where he is currently the reserve-team manager and also works with the first team. He initially coached the 'B' team and has also coached Everton teams to victory in the FA Youth Cup and FA Premier Reserve League, North Section.

Rick Holden: For the last 14 years, he has been based on the Isle of Man, where he has a chartered physiotherapy practice based at Peel Football Club. He also manages the club. He had a short spell at Barnsley, where he was assistant manager/physio when Andy Ritchie was in charge there.

Denis Irwin: Is still heavily involved at Manchester United, where he is an MUTV pundit and a match-day host in the hospitality suites. In addition, he writes a weekly column for the Irish paper Sunday World and has various other media commitments.

WHERE ARE THEY NOW?

Norman Kelly: Has recently returned to his native Belfast after coaching in America for a number of years. He is Sports Development Officer at The Hanwood Sports Centre, a 3G football and gymnasium complex which opened earlier this year.

Chris Makin: The former right-back is based in Stockport after, during his career, building up a property portfolio which he now looks after since his retirement two years ago.

Ian Marshall: Is due to return to these shores anytime from Newfoundland, Canada, which has been his home for the last five years. He has run soccer schools and camps and also organised football tours, bringing parties to England. He also ran a restaurant, Sam's Place, which was named after his wife, for a number of years.

Scott McGarvey: The former striker has been a football agent for the last 12 years and currently has about 35 players on the books of his company Mac1 Sports. Previously, he had a spell selling pitch sand to football clubs, including Latics.

MARVELLOUS MILLIE......keeping a close eye on his man in the FA Cup semi-final.

Mike Milligan: Is an entrepreneur with various interests, including a YouTube-style internet company www.playfactor.tv. He also does corporate work, mainly in the Norwich area where he lives, as well as giving advice to grass-roots football.

Simon Mooney: Is the only member of the 1989/90 squad whose whereabouts are not known, though he is thought to have family in the Heywood area.

Paul Moulden: The striker severed his links with football after retiring, buying a fish-and-chip shop at Great Lever, Bolton. He has since moved to a similar eaterie at Tonge Fold, Bolton, and has a hands-on role in the business. He has endured health problems, having two new hips and last year suffering a brain haemorrhage.

Roger Palmer: Is as elusive now as he was during his playing days and it was a major exercise tracking him down to Sale, where he now lives in retirement.

Neil Redfearn: After playing until he was 41, he became assistant boss at York City. Today, he is employed full-time by Leeds United as coach to their under-18s.

Andy Rhodes: Is goalkeeping coach at Preston North End, having previously been reunited with Joe Royle at Ipswich Town. There was also a spell working with the keepers at Boundary Park when Andy Ritchie was in charge.

Andy Ritchie: Since retiring, he has had a mix of management and media jobs. He has been at the helm at Boundary Park as well as Huddersfield and Barnsley. He does not rule out a return to football, but is happy as a BBC Radio Leeds and MUTV pundit as well as writing a weekly blog for the Football League website.

Andy Ritchie – still open-minded about returning to football despite his media duties.

Paul Warhurst: Having retired from playing two years ago aged 38, he has become an agent employed by First Artists, the London-based company which represented him during his playing days.

Gary Williams: He and his family kicked off a new life three years ago in Spain, where he does seasonal work in a restaurant, with wife Melanie as cook. Previously he was licensee of the Horse and Groom, one of three pubs he ran in his native Bristol.

Subscribers

Graham Anderson
David Brierley
Cliff Butler
Giacomo Cavallino
Janet Chadwick
Howard Clarke
Michael Clarke
Gary Davies
Yvonne Davies
Mike Dunkerley
Chris England
Peter Gartside (AGS Electrical Ltd)
Barry and Joyce Griffiths
Andrew Thomas Halliwell
Alan Hardy
Ian Hill
Norman Holden
John Kelso
Tracy Knuckey
Alan Miller
Mike Newton
David Nuttall
Barry Owen
Jeff Pickett
John Shepherd
Rev John Simmons
Sinbad
John Slevin
Peter Smith
Andrew & Kevin Steel
Derek R Taylor
Janet Taylor
Rob Thorne & Danielle Sullivan
Andrew & Ann Thorne
Sylvia Turner
Franny Ward

Autographs

The PFA

Chris Powell , PFA Chairman (Leicester City FC)

"For the good of the game"

- Disciplinary representation
- Contract advice
- Dispute resolution
- Coaching
- Commercial
- Legal advice
- Medical Insurance
- Hardship grants
- Insurance with regard to permanent total disability
- Physical and addictive rehabilitation
- Non-contributory pension scheme & death benefit
- Financial advice
- Education and vocational training
- Community & charity initiatives
- Equity, diversity and anti-racism

Head Office 0161-236-0575
London Office 0207-236-5148
Email: info@thepfa.co.uk

www.givemefootball.com

Dr. Kershaw's Hospice

Turf Lane
Royton, Oldham
Lancashire
OL2 6EU

Reg Charity No. 1105924

Tel: 0161 624 2727 (Switchboard)
Tel: 0161 624 9984 (Appeals Office)
Fax: 0161 628 3951 (Appeals Office)
Email: appeals@drkershawshospice.org.uk
Website: www.drkershawshospice.org.uk
Tel: 0161 624 9213 (Hospice Lottery)
Tel: 01706 290973 (Hospice Shops)

Dr Kershaw's Hospice provides specialist palliative care for adults with non-curable life-limiting illnesses in a peaceful and homely environment.

The services that we provide include:

- 12 inpatient 24 hour care places
- 15 day care places per day (5 days per week)
- Acupuncture clinic
- Aromatherapy service

- Beautician service
- Bereavement support service
- Lymphoedema clinic
- Pain relief clinic

As a charity we depend very heavily on the generosity of our supporters and only receive a fraction of our annual costs from the local Primary Care Trust. **All of our services are provided free of charge.**

The running costs for the year 2009/10 will be £1.7 million, of which £1.1 million must be raised independently, through the Appeals Office - events, campaigns, donations, legacies, Friends of the Hospice, Hospice Lottery, shops etc. This equates to around £4,650 per day to enable the Hospice to remain open. Without this vital funding, we would not be able to maintain the excellent level of service that we currently provide.

Fundraising

A variety of fundraising events are held throughout the year in support of the Hospice. For example, the Hospice to Hospice and Midnight sponsored walks are annual events which take place in April and June respectively. Other annual events include the Gala Ball, Sportman's Dinner and Man of Oldham event. Home and public collection boxes also play a significant fundraising role for the Hospice. For details of our latest events please visit our website or to request a collection box please contact the Appeals Office.

The Hospice Lottery

The Hospice Lottery was launched in October 2003 and makes a large contribution to the funding of the Hospice. By joining the Hospice Lottery, and contributing £1 per week, not only will you have the chance to win our weekly top prize of £1,000 or one of five runner up prizes of £50, but you will be helping to provide vital services to our local community. All profits from the Lottery go directly to the Hospice. There are several payment options available; credit/debit card, standing order, cheque and postal order. If you are interested in joining the Lottery, please download an application form from our website at www.drkershawshospice.org/LotteryForm.pdf or alternatively contact our Hotline on 0870 241 3495 or the Lottery Office at the Hospice on 0161 624 9213.

Friends of the Hospice

The 'Friends of Dr Kershaw's' was launched in November 1991 and is very important to the Hospice. Sadly, as is the case with most charities, for various reasons, the membership has dwindled and new friends are urgently needed. For as little as £10 you can become a Friend of Dr Kershaw's Hospice. In return, you will receive a regular newsletter, a lapel badge and other items of interest throughout the year. We are hoping to sign up 1,000 new Friends in 2010. In order to become a Friend of the Hospice please contact the Appeals Office to receive a form via the post or download an application form from our website at www.drkershawshospice.org.uk/Friendsform.pdf

Hospice Shops

The Hospice has four charity shops (Shaw (two branches), Royton and Lees) that sell a variety of goods including; clothes, toys, books, cds/records/cassettes and bric-a-brac. Donations of good quality, second hand or new items are always gratefully received. The Hospice also has an eBay shop at http://myworld.ebay.co.uk/drkershawshospice

If you would like to find out more about Dr. Kershaw's Hospice or would like to make a donation, please visit our website at www.drkershawshospice.org.uk. All donations are greatly appreciated.